This book is for pilgrims of disillusionment and even despair. It is for the worn down, brokenhearted disciple who has learned the weight of the cross that leads first to death, and only then to life. It is hope for the despondent, encouragement for the weary, and a soothing salve for the tattered and torn. An important message about the inevitability of change, *Road to Transformation* is a poignant perspective on transition and how God uses difficult seasons to reveal Himself to us in ways we might not recognize otherwise. There is a distinct difference between a crossroad and the end of the road, and Barnes serves as a veteran voice from the other side with the resounding message, "Journey on!"

—Mickey Davis
Former Pastor, Grace Community Church
Salem, Missouri

Within these pages are more than sentences and chapters, but instead you will find a launching pad ignited by the Holy Spirit to proceed in your own journey of transformation.

—Trent Morgan
Pastor, Grace Community Church
Salem, Missouri

After reading Rhonda's unique insight, it is evident that she has received tremendous revelation from the Holy Spirit. I am convinced that anyone who reads this book will be able to identify their own spot on their road to transformation. From her personal experiences to her impressive explanation of the scripture, she leaves you with hope, and with the ability to see the bigger picture on your journey with the Lord. I am confident that whoever reads the words in this book will have a renewed mentality that assures you that whether you are in construction, a detour, a highway, or a back road on your road to transformation, God will inevitably help you arrive to your final destination. This book has helped me refocus my sights on where I am going, but also to be content with the journey. This book will be an incredible help to all who read it.

—Daniel R. Tidmore
Staff Evangelist, Grace Community Church
Salem, Missouri

Road
to
Transformation

RHONDA BARNES

Road
to
Transformation

Journey to God's Glory

CHALFANT ECKERT
PUBLISHING

ISBN: 978-1-63308-125-3 (paperback)
ISBN: 978-1-63308-126-0 (ebook)

Cover & Interior Design by R'tor John D. Maghuyop

Scriptures:
Unless otherwise noted, scriptures quoted are from the
NASU translation of the Holy Bible.

CHALFANT ECKERT
PUBLISHING

1028 S Bishop Avenue, Dept. 178
Rolla, MO 65401

Printed in United States of America

DEDICATION

The *Road to Transformation* is dedicated to

Tammy Davis
February 14, 1960 – January 8, 2007

Tammy was our pastor's wife and the leader of our worship team. She taught us the importance of praise and worship as a means of ushering in the presence of God in a corporate gathering. She was such an amazing, inspiring role model and friend.

TABLE OF CONTENTS

ACKNOWLEDGMENTS

First and foremost, I would like to thank the Lord for empowering me to write this book. Without the revelation the Holy Spirit provides, I would have nothing to say.

Secondly, I would like to express my sincere appreciation and love to my two best friends and soul sisters, Christa Barnes and Felecia Stienbarger. Thank you both for always being my spiritual support, and for dreaming with me. I am so thankful that I have your company as we continue to pursue the deep and bottomless things God has for us!

I could not be who I am today without the love and support of my family. My husband Dennis; my children, Tyler and Nicole; their spouses, Kylie and Willie; and my grandsons, Titus and Isaac. I love all of you deeply.

I want to acknowledge Christa Barnes for her editing support. Thank you for providing clarity and accuracy.

I am extremely thankful for the divine connection with Dr. Kitty Bickford and her team at Chalfant Eckert Publishing. This group played an important role assisting me in making my dream a reality.

Finally, I would like to thank the current and former leadership, and congregation of Grace Community Church in Salem, Missouri, for your support, guidance, and love throughout the years.

INTRODUCTION

I want to engage your imagination for one brief moment. Suppose you are sitting in your vehicle parked at the extreme edge of the West Coast of the United States, and you want to travel to the farthest point on the East Coast. If you are like me, you would put the address of your final destination into your GPS so you have a map to follow, and turn-by-turn instruction spoken to you along the way.

Depending on the route you choose, the stops you make, the speed you travel, and the obstacles along the way, this journey of about 3,000 miles could take as little as 45 hours for some, and may never be completed for others.

We will use this trip as an example of one possible map of the *Road to Transformation* that one could travel on. The road is different for each individual but I guarantee you will be able to relate to some of the stops and experiences on the journey, if not at this phase in life, at some other point.

The inspiration for this book came several years ago while traveling a very curvy road in a rural part of Missouri. At that time in my career, I was traveling between three locations as a manager. During one of those early morning three hour commutes, I had an unusual experience.

While driving, the road before me faded to the background, and I began to see the pages of a book. I saw the cover and I saw the word *Transformation*. I saw the font and many chapter titles. Thirty minutes later, after many details became vivid pictures in my mind, I realized I had driven several miles and did not remember the road or how I got from where I was at the beginning of this experience to my current location.

Over the course of the last nine years since that encounter, I have had many detours and roadblocks in making this book a reality. Even though I had the GPS set to my desired destination, I have often heard the voice say, "Turn around when possible," or "Rerouting in progress." I have tried to start the project many times in my own strength, but it was during the nine years since that original experience that my personal journey led me to the portion of my own road to transformation in which I experienced the majority of the stops we will discuss in this book.

As stated earlier, a 3,000-mile trip from the West to the East Coast could take as little as 45 hours. Each individual will choose a unique route with unique stops and excursions along the way. Some delays are by choice, some are results of decisions, and some are totally out of one's control. The same concept was true for the Children of Israel. The Bible tells us in Deuteronomy 1:2 that their journey to the promise land should have taken no more than eleven days, but it took them 40 years. As I was preparing for the New Year, the Lord gave me a revelation about the significance of moving forward from 2013 into 2014 using this example:

When the Children of Israel were ready to go from the old into the new after 40 long years, the first obstacle on their forward path to the Promised Land was Jericho. In the Bible, the destruction of Jericho is stamped with the number thirteen. When Joshua directed the priests to carry the Ark into the Jordan River and the water parted for the Children of Israel to move forward on dry land, there was an opportunity to look back and remember how God had delivered them when they crossed the Red Sea on dry land also. However, this time they were not running from an enemy, they were running toward their enemy, and they were going to move forward to possess everything promised to them.

In order to overcome the city of Jericho they were instructed to march around the impenetrable walls once each day for six days, and seven times on the seventh day, making thirteen times in all. When that thirteenth lap was complete and the priest blew the trumpet, Joshua instructed them to shout. In that moment everything changed, those walls came crashing down making a bridge into their future.

The number fourteen is also significant in the Bible. Many agree it represents a double anointing, or a double measure of spiritual perfection. For me personally, and for the corporate body which I am a part of, there was a special significance in ending 2013 and beginning 2014 worshiping our King.

People choose many different types of activities during the moment the clock strikes midnight signifying the end of one year and beginning of the next. This year, many of the people in my church family, including me, chose to use that moment to sing praises and worship the Almighty God!

I believe God took note of that choice and for me personally, at the end of 2013, the walls obstructing the divine destinations I was traveling towards came crashing down! I believe that our expressions of worship to the King of Kings and our shouts at midnight marked the moment in the spiritual realm that the walls came down and created a bridge into the next dimension of His power and His glory. A new day had dawned.

There is something about leaving behind the old year and beginning a new one that is so refreshing. The end of a year is a great time to reevaluate and reprioritize. Looking back over the past year is an opportunity to assess and review the year's accomplishments and rejoice in the victories, but it is also a great time for putting all the past frustrations, disappointments, and failures behind us and focusing on the new.

My personal forward path is marked with the completion of this book. With God's help, I hope to articulate some of the spiritual truths He has revealed to me while travelling along this road of transformation. The enemy of our soul wants to get us off the desired path God has for each of us, or cause delays such as the Children of Israel experienced. My goal is that you will discover those tactics and move past any roadblock that is hindering you from fulfilling your unique destiny. Buckle up and let's go!

Chapter 1

Departure Time

Long before time existed, God had a plan for each of us. God knew our names enough to write them down before the foundations of the earth were set (Revelation 13:8). We often refer to this fact as our destiny. If you are destined, you are directed with purpose. Destined individuals are destination driven, which essentially means they are on a road journeying somewhere. The question is, "Do you know where you are going?"

In God's divine design, He looked down through time and specifically created you to be alive on this earth for such a time as this. It doesn't matter the circumstances under which you were born, God chose you from countless possibilities to be here now. Every living soul is conceived with a God-given purpose embedded in their DNA. You can be sure that He has an explicit purpose in mind for your life.

> *For You formed my inward parts; You wove me in my mother's womb. I will give thanks to You, for I am fearfully and wonderfully made; wonderful are Your works, and my soul knows it very well. My frame was not hidden from You, when I was made in secret and*

skillfully wrought in the depths of the earth; Your eyes
have seen my unformed substance; and in Your book were
all written the days that were ordained for me, when as
yet there was not one of them. How precious also are Your
thoughts of me, O God!

Psalm 139: 13-17

Our destiny is not just about a place, it is about the process and the journey. As we embark on this trip, one of my desires is that you learn to embrace with grace the place He has for you in this race. Every part of the journey is important. We often fail to realize the significance of every experience along the way.

Under Construction

One absolute certainty is that every person who travels long enough will eventually encounter road construction. I remember when construction work on highways was limited to certain seasons and specific times of the day. With improved processes and equipment, this is no longer the case. The same is true on our *Road to Transformation*. Construction zones often appear when we least expect them, and when we do not have the time or patience to be delayed by them. For example, several years ago, the highway I traveled on daily for twenty-eight miles needed significant repair. Each day as I traveled this road and watched the progress of the construction during my commute, God unfolded more revelation to me about this process I refer to as the road to transformation.

There was a plan for this highway construction long before I even realized it was to begin. Key individuals were responsible for developing the timeline, the funding, and the blueprint. I remember watching pieces of the construction plan unfold and not understanding how it would fit in the final plan, but at the end of the process, it all made sense.

Similar to the construction plan, God has a plan for His church, or His corporate body, and He has a plan for each individual in the body. Long ago He established the timeline, settled how the cost would be paid, and developed the blueprint.

> *For My thoughts are not your thoughts, neither are your ways My ways, says the Lord. For as the heavens are higher than the earth, so are my ways higher than your ways and My thoughts than your thoughts....So shall My word be that goes forth out of My mouth: it shall not return to me void [without producing any effect, useless], but it shall accomplish that which I please and purpose, and it shall prosper in the thing for which I sent it.*
>
> Isaiah 55:8-9; 11 AMP

His thoughts and ways are much higher than our human ability to understand. That is why it is so amazing that when we receive Jesus Christ as our Lord and Savior, the Holy Spirit takes residence inside us and provides us with divine insight! One of my former pastors always said, "Hang around with the Holy Spirit, and He will make you smart!" The Holy Spirit helps us stay in step with God's perfect plan for our lives. He comes with power and spiritual gifts that you can read about in 1 Corinthians 12-14. We have had countless opportunities in our local church to record words of prophecy or interpretation of tongues when they were manifested and I will share some of these "Words" with you now and in future chapters. These Words are powerful because His thoughts and ways are higher than our human reasoning.

One such Word was about this very subject of the construction zone we travel through on our road to transformation:

> "…And those things that you walk through are not those things to cause you to stumble and to fall. But those things that you walk through are those things that will strengthen you, and it's those circumstances that you walk through, that you will see that I am with you, and I am a strong tower, and you can walk and live in the confidence that what you are going through, I am going with you. For I am with you always, and what you think at this moment will bring destruction, I declare to you, that what you are going through is part of the process that I have designed for you to bring construction into your life. Those things that the enemy means for harm, I will prove to you that they will work for your good and My glory if you will trust in Me with all of your heart. Lean not unto your own understanding. Set your sight upon Me. I am the author and I am the finisher of your faith, and I will perfect those things and keep those things that you have committed to me against the day just like you are walking through. Trust in the Lord, lean upon Him and He will bring to pass those things that He has spoken."

God has a plan! He has a plan for His corporate body and He has a plan for you as an individual.

> *For I know the thoughts and plans that I have for you, says the Lord, thoughts and plans for welfare and peace and not for evil, to give you hope in your final outcome.*
> Jeremiah 29:11, AMP

If we are going to see His plan in action, we have to yield to the process of transformation.

Yield to the Process

The title of this book is *Road to Transformation*, but what is transformation? Let me explain it the way God revealed this truth to me. First, it is a process. It does not happen overnight and I personally believe it does not end until we pass from this life to the next one.

During a study of 2 Corinthians 3:18, I noticed a different word choice in each of the following three translations of the Bible. I bold the words for emphasis below:

> *But we all, with open face beholding as in a glass the glory of the Lord, are **changed** into the same image from glory to glory, even as by the Spirit of the Lord.*
>
> 2 Corinthians 3:18 KJV

> *But we all, with unveiled face, beholding as in a mirror the glory of the Lord, are being **transformed** into the same image from glory to glory, just as by the Spirit of the Lord.*
>
> 2 Corinthians 3:18 NKJV

> *And all of us, as with unveiled face, [because we] continue to behold [in the Word of God] as in a mirror the glory of the Lord, are constantly being **transfigured** into His very own image in ever increasing splendor and from one degree of glory to another; [for this come] from the Lord [Who is] the Spirit.*
>
> 2 Corinthians 3:18 AMP

These three different translations encouraged me to study those word choices. The first version used the word "changed" which means to become different. When I think of something changing, one of the best examples is water changing to ice when it is in a very cold environment. However, the interesting thing about this example is that when the temperature is altered back to a warm environment, the ice changes back to water.

The second translation chose the word "transformed." When I think about that word, the best example that comes to mind is a caterpillar transforming into a butterfly. It is a lengthy process, but it is permanent. Once the caterpillar exits the cocoon, no environmental change will make it return to its former state. It is a total transformation process that modifies everything about the caterpillar from how it looks initially to how it moves from place to place.

The third translation expounds on the second. The word choice here is "transfigured." Merriam-Webster online dictionary defines it as "giving a new and typically exalted or spiritual appearance to" (2014). If we continue to yield to the process, God will not only change us, He will transform and transfigure us into a new creation. I do not want to be guilty of changing with my environment. I want to yield to the transformation process that God has designed for me personally, so I can be transfigured into a creation He intends for me to become.

As we yield to the process, we must move forward out of transition and into transformation. Be mindful, however, that the transformation process takes place in degrees. The following is another prophetic Word shared at our church about this truth.

> *"For the Lord would say unto you this day do not be dismayed, and do not be discouraged concerning this journey you are making. For did I not say that this*

transformation process would take place by degrees? Did I not say that you are changed and transformed from one degree of glory to the next? A degree may seem so minute, like such a small step, but in the natural realm of navigation, degrees determine your destination. Degrees determine your destination, and so it is in the spiritual realm, one degree's difference can alter your direction. One degree's difference can cause you to miss the mark. So do not despise these days of degrees, for I have started the work, and I am able to finish it, and I will bring you to the place that I have ordained, saith the Lord."

When my nephew was small, his parents were traveling home from St. Louis, Missouri, during a major construction on I-44. They had been sitting in one place on the interstate for a long time. My nephew, from his car seat, saw the outer road, and said to his parents, "I wish we were over on that road!"

When a highway department determines to expand from a two-lane road to a four-lane road, often travelers will be required to endure a one-lane road for a season. Waiting is one of the most difficult parts of a construction zone. My former pastor said the Lord asked him once, "Will you wait while I work, or will you work while I wait?"

People can easily go off course during the transformation process. Even when it is tempting to take the path of least resistance, or to detour from the predetermined route, stay the course! There is a story that describes this concept well:

> "A man found a cocoon of a butterfly. One day a small opening appeared. He sat and watched the butterfly for several hours as it struggled to force its body through that little hole. Then it seemed to stop making any progress. It appeared as if it had gotten as far as it could, and it could go no further.

So the man decided to help the butterfly. He took a pair of scissors and snipped off the remaining bit of the cocoon. The butterfly then emerged easily. But it had a swollen body and small, shriveled wings.

The man continued to watch the butterfly because he expected that, at any moment, the wings would enlarge and expand to be able to support the body, which would contract in time.

Neither happened! In fact, the butterfly spent the rest of its life crawling around with a swollen body and shriveled wings. It was never able to fly.

What the man, in his kindness and haste did not understand, was that the restricting cocoon and the struggle required to get through the tiny opening were God's way of forcing fluid from the body of the butterfly into its wings. It would then be ready for flight once it achieved its freedom from the cocoon."

Author unknown

This kind man failed to understand that the process of transformation is critical. Even though transformation can be painful at times, we must stay on course and allow the process to complete.

As stated earlier, the initial revelation of this book began with the construction that was occurring on the twenty-eight mile stretch of highway I traveled every day between my home community and the city where I worked. This construction process had several distinct phases. It was determined that the majority of the road, about a sixteen-mile section in the middle, should be totally replaced. The work to clear the path, create the foundation, and eventually build the new road was lengthy, but it did not seem very invasive. It did not affect travel much because it was being built along the side of the old road. The difference however, was obvious when it was complete. The new portion of road was so comfortable in comparison to the old that I was able to use cruise control on this rural road for the first time.

After the initial phase of the plan was complete, it seemed like all progress stopped. I remember driving this route day after day and wondering if they would ever complete the project. Then one day they began the work again. It was an eight-mile stretch of highway that had to be reconstructed in order to connect with the new one. The first four miles of this section seemed painless, except for the delays, as this portion was expanded to a four-lane road. It was the last four miles of this segment that opened my eyes to the sacrifices for this new road.

This was a heavily populated part of the highway. People had to give up their homes. I remember driving by every day and watching those houses as they were taken apart piece by piece. After the project was completed, we could clearly see the destination, but we could also look back and see the process that got us there.

This example of the different phases of construction is a perfect picture of our journey to transformation. During the process, there are path clearing, foundation laying, and building phases that we often do not see happening because our daily activities do not seem altered by them. However, there are zones where the waiting seems endless and the sacrifice is great. There are also times when it is difficult to understand how point A could ever intersect with point B, similar to the way it was difficult for me to understand how the new highway could ever connect with the old one. God will often show you phase one and phase five in the plan for your own life, but you have to exercise trust and faith as you slowly progress through the process in between.

One of my favorite scriptures is:

Call to Me and I will answer you and show you great and mighty things, fenced in and hidden, which you do not know (do not distinguish and recognize, have knowledge of and understand).

Jeremiah 33:3, AMP

If Jeremiah could learn these things, I believe they are available to us as well. I believe these are the very things that will take us beyond change to transformation. However, just as the progress of the new road costs something, most transformation will also come with a price.

There are times when I go shopping and I will see something I like, but when I see the price tag, I sometimes determine that I do not like it that much! The deep and hidden things of God are not free. Jesus paid the ultimate price for us to have access to these things, but individually it will cost us something.

One way to see this concept is to consider the seating dynamics in a theater or a stadium. All seats are arranged to see the event as it occurs, however, the view from some seats is much better than others. In fact, some have special booths or box seats that provide the very best opportunity to enjoy the event. What is the difference with these seats? The difference is the cost! If you want better seats, you will pay the higher price.

When we talk about the price on our journey to transformation, the cost will likely include something we never seem to have enough of, and that is our time. It may cost you your reputation, an activity you really enjoy, your sleep, or your favorite television show. The question is, "How badly do you want the best seat in the house to watch the fenced in and hidden things of God being revealed?"

Rhonda Barnes

SLOW – Proceed With Caution

I travel a lot, and during these times there have been many revelations deposited in my spirit. At times, my eyes have been opened to the literal road as a picture of the journey to transformation. It is not a straight road, and there is no easy way to get there. It is a long road and often requires a slow pace because of hindrances, which get in the way with no opportunity to pass them. In the same context as overtaking another car, it is not safe to try and rush past these obstacles ahead when you cannot see what might be coming towards you from around the curve or over the hill, which could inevitably destroy you if you are in the wrong lane. We are cautioned to take the necessary precautions and not act on impulse alone to get around what is directly in front of us. The fact is that many individuals have set their course to drive in the opposite direction of transformation. The enemy would like to use those driving in the opposite direction of traffic to permanently throw us off course. Not every obstacle in our way should provoke us to go faster.

The lesson to learn here is that sometimes obstacles are not true hindrances. Sometimes it is an opportunity to slow down because there is something to see, something to hear, or perhaps touch, that you would miss if you were traveling at your preferred speed.

Another obstacle to avoid is keeping your focus on the rearview mirror for too long. That mirror is there to provide safety checks but if you continue in forward motion with your focus behind you, it will not take long for a collision to happen.

We should learn from the story of Lot and his wife (See Genesis 19). God was about to destroy the city of Sodom and Gomorrah. He sent angels to lead Lot and his family to safety. They were instructed not to look back, but Lot's wife did not heed the warning and was turned into a pillar of salt. What was she leaving behind that would cause her to disobey God's command? Very often we know what is behind us, and find comfort in holding on to that. Releasing it and embracing a future of uncertainties may prove a little difficult to do. The lesson to learn is we cannot give God our yesterdays, so we need to focus on our todays and tomorrows. We can learn from our past but we cannot change it, so we must move forward.

We often miss today because we are so focused on tomorrow, or we are still living in yesterday. We need to enjoy where we are on the way to where we are going. It is a journey!

Chapter 2

THE FIRST LEG OF THE JOURNEY

I have had numerous opportunities to travel long trips, some of which have lasted more than eight hours. Looking back on these times, it is the first leg of these journeys that seem to be the easiest. Initially, in the early stages of the trip, there is excitement about reaching the destination. There is a heightened expectation about what lies ahead. Driving, as well as being a passenger, is more enjoyable at the beginning of a long drive. But then, eventually, fatigue, weariness, and the reality of how long the trip really is sets in.

This same concept essentially describes the beginning of your spiritual journey as well. In the beginning, the road and the vision is clear, expectations are grand, and there is an amazing sense of purpose for the new life that lies before you. There is energy, unction, and a new level of boldness you have never known before. The promises of God fuel passion in you that you never knew existed. It is a time of revival.

Revival is a term that is often used to describe a time of special services at a church. But this is a very skewed and inaccurate definition of the term. When I use the word 'revival' I am not referring to a 'special service.' *Microsoft Encarta Dictionary* (2009) defines revival in several ways:

- ✓ "Process of reviving somebody; the process of bringing somebody back to life, consciousness, or full strength.
- ✓ Renewal of interest; a renewal of interest in something that results in its becoming popular once more.
- ✓ Renewed religious interest; a new interest in religion, or the reawakening to such interest."

I worked in a hospital setting for 20 years as a Respiratory Therapist. I have assisted and watched many individuals being "revived" from a state of clinical death. If the process of being revived is not administered, then clinical death can lead to biological death. Many of these people went on to live healthy lives after being revived following their near death experience.

This is the kind of "revival" I am referring to. I believe there are so many Christians walking around in a spiritually dead state similar to clinical death in the natural, and unfortunately, most are not even aware of it. The kind of revival I am speaking of renews interest in the things of God, but more importantly, it connects or more so reconnects the individual with the giver of life in a spiritual life-sustaining way!

For many this journey begins when they accept the Lord Jesus Christ as their personal savior. For me this journey really began years after I became a Christian. Even as a small child, I was always interested in the things of God. I never doubted His existence. Through my teenage and young adult years, I served God passionately and to the best of my ability. You can be saved and participate in church, but have never really had a genuine encounter with the true presence of God. Such an encounter will change you. I feel that my true spiritual journey did not really begin until I was in my early thirties. This was when I experienced God in a new and powerful way, and it marked me in such a way that I felt like my road to transformation actually began at this point.

It was at this time in my life that I heard about the amazing revival that was happening in Pensacola, Florida. I saw a couple videos of services where countless numbers of people were being saved, delivered, set free, and forever changed by the power of God. While I knew that God was all-powerful, I had never seen anything like this in my lifetime. I desperately wanted to be a part of what God was doing.

A friend and I planned to attend the National Quartet Convention and she asked if I was interested in taking a few extra days and going to Pensacola first. I was all in! I left on that thirteen-hour road trip with no idea that my life was about to change.

The first thing I observed at that meeting was the unbelievable hunger that people had which caused them to gather as much as twelve hours before scheduled service times just to get a seat in the main auditorium. We were fortunate to get seats both nights we were there. People were hungry for God.

I must admit that at first I was a bit distracted just watching the unique responses from thousands of people as they experienced the manifested presence of God at this level. In all of my years of serving God, I had never felt anything like it. I knew that I was at the right place, at the perfect time. The presence of God saturated the place to a degree that I have never known or experienced in my life. You see, you cannot miss what you have never had. But once you have experienced it, there is absolutely no going back.

I strongly believe that an individual cannot encounter the presence of God in this way without being transformed. I have not been the same since those first two days I spent at the Brownsville Revival. The wonderful thing is that it did not end there. It was simply the first leg of the journey for me! But I knew that there was no going back.

I noticed when I returned home that things that used to be important to me were not very significant anymore. I noticed that television shows I previously enjoyed watching were no longer a good use of my time. I found myself wanting to finish all of my responsibilities as quickly as possible so I could spend more time with God. I had a deep insatiable hunger for more of God that could only be satisfied by Him. I could not get enough. I wanted so much more.

Worship, prayer, and Bible study all took on new meaning. I longed to experience the presence of God as I did in Florida, and I was willing to pay the price. My hunger led me to meet with my pastor and ask if we could start a prayer time on Saturday nights at the church to intercede for God to visit us in a similar way as in Brownsville. I knew that if God showed up there, He can show up anywhere. It is the same God we claim to serve and there is no reason why we should deny ourselves experiencing His life changing presence.

We quickly discovered that if you seek Him, you will find Him (Jeremiah 29:13). We learned many things about how to pray through the Spirit. We also realized that prayer is not always easy. We learned that giving up our Saturday nights to go to the church and pray was often sacrificial, but for 17 years, that is exactly what we did. We paid the price, and God honored His word.

I can honestly say that those nights in prayer played a significant role in my personal road to transformation. There were many times that the presence of God just filled the church in unbelievable ways when we met to pray. These types of encounters have caused me to passionately and relentlessly pursue times in His presence.

We see many examples in both the Old and the New Testament where individuals were dramatically transformed by the presence of God. Moses is a perfect example:

> *Now Moses was pasturing the flock of Jethro his father-in-law, the priest of Midian; and he led the flock to the west side of the wilderness and came to Horeb, the mountain of God. The angel of the Lord appeared to him in a blazing fire from the midst of a bush; and he looked, and behold, the bush was burning with fire, yet the bush was not consumed. So Moses said, "I must turn aside now and see this marvelous sight, why the bush is not burned up." When the Lord saw that he turned aside to look, God called to him from the midst of the bush and said, "Moses, Moses!" And he said, "Here I am." Then He said, "Do not come near here; remove your sandals from your feet, for the place on which you are standing is holy ground." He said also, "I am the God of your father, the God of Abraham, the God of Isaac, and the God of Jacob." Then Moses hid his face, for he was afraid to look at God....*
>
> *And He said, "Certainly I will be with you, and this shall be the sign to you that it is I who have sent you: when you have brought the people out of Egypt, you shall worship God at this mountain." Then Moses said to God, "Behold, I am going to the sons of Israel, and I will say to them, 'The God of your fathers has sent me to you.' Now they may say to me, 'What is His name?' What shall I say*

to them?" God said to Moses, "I AM WHO I AM"; and
He said, "Thus you shall say to the sons of Israel, 'I AM
has sent me to you.'"

Exodus 3:1-6; 12-14

God calls Himself *"I am who I am!"* In the original Hebrew language, the word used is *Yahweh*. This Hebrew phrase is indicating action. What God is saying to Moses is that He desires to be a God who is present! Yahweh is the promise of the living presence of God Himself day by day with His people! (Faith, 1995).

I will walk among you and be your God, and you shall
be my people.

Leviticus 26:12

Moses was a different man after the burning bush experience. This was the beginning of an intimate relationship with his Father. It was his experience with the presence of God that empowered Moses to push past obstacles to follow the directions God gave him. When you truly encounter God, you begin to perceive obstacles in a different light. Even after God began to use him mightily with signs, wonders, and leading the Children of Israel out of Egypt, he continued to seek time in the presence of God. He was never truly satisfied with yesterday's experiences. It was his relentless passion that resulted in God sitting him down and telling him how the world begun so the book of Genesis could be recorded. It was these types of encounters that gave him divine direction for how to continue on his journey.

Now Moses used to take the tent and pitch it outside the
camp, a good distance from the camp, and he called it

the tent of meeting. And everyone who sought the Lord would go out to the tent of meeting which was outside the camp. And it came about, whenever Moses went out to the tent, that all the people would arise and stand, each at the entrance of his tent, and gaze after Moses until he entered the tent. Whenever Moses entered the tent, the pillar of cloud would descend and stand at the entrance of the tent; and the Lord would speak with Moses. When all the people saw the pillar of cloud standing at the entrance of the tent, all the people would arise and worship, each at the entrance of his tent. Thus the Lord used to speak to Moses face to face, just as a man speaks to his friend. When Moses returned to the camp, his servant Joshua, the son of Nun, a young man, would not depart from the tent.

Exodus 33:7-11

If you continue reading this text, you find where Moses said to the Lord, *"If Your presence does not go with us, do not lead us up from here."* (Exodus 33:15). Seeking the presence of God was Moses' top priority. He urged a group of people to understand this focus, and while some did not seem to embrace the importance of a "presence-led" lifestyle, his future successor certainly did. Notice that Joshua, as a young man, would not leave the tent! I believe God took notice of this, and began preparing him to take Moses' place and be the one to lead the Children of Israel into the Promised Land.

David was another great leader in the Old Testament. I believe he was different because he learned at an early age how to usher in the presence of God through worship. He was a passionate man. We can learn much about his focus from his writings. The Psalms form a rich book of inspiration and passion from the heart of a true worshipper.

One thing I have asked from the Lord, that I shall seek:
That I may dwell in the house of the Lord all the days of
my life, To behold the beauty of the Lord And to meditate
in His temple.

Psalm 27:4

You hide them in the secret place of Your presence from the
conspiracies of man;

Psalm 31:20a

As for me, You uphold me in my integrity, And You set me
in Your presence forever.

Psalm 41:12

Do not cast me away from Your presence and do not take
Your Holy Spirit from me.

Psalm 51:11

A dramatic transformation by the presence of God is not limited to Old Testament examples. One of the greatest instances in the New Testament is found in Acts 9-13 where Saul, a man known for the persecution of the church is radically transformed by the power of God. Saul, later known as Paul, went on to write most of the New Testament after his encounter with Jesus.

After many years of prayer, our church began to have these types of encounters with the presence and power of God. It is interesting how visiting ministers began to comment about how unique the presence of God was and still is in our church. We received a prophetic Word during a service that we have continued to claim as a promise for our corporate body:

"My church, have I not declared in My word, in times of old, that I have performed many mighty, many powerful works in the sight of My children, Israel? Did they not stand back in awe? Did they not stand back in amazement? Did they not stand back and declare, 'We have never seen it after this fashion before'? Well I say unto you this day, that those mighty works that I performed for My children Israel, so in like manner shall I also perform them for this assembly, so that you might stand back in awe, so that you might stand back in amazement, so that you might declare My power and My glory, and give Me praise, saith the Lord of hosts!"

It is impossible to share every powerful moment that has caused us to stand back in awe, but I want to attempt to articulate a few. I believe one of the most pivotal encounters with the power of God, which literally marked us as a corporate body, happened in late December, 2003. We were having revival meetings between the winter holidays. The power of God was visiting our church in such a unique way that I wrote in my journal, "We will forever be changed!" In this particular service, the man who was preaching looked at our pastor, who was sitting on the front pew at the time, and made a statement about how he had always carried the water, but now the water would carry him. When he made that statement, the power of God literally paralyzed our pastor for about five hours. This encounter with the presence of God empowered our leader in a new way to guide us through an amazing time of renewal. He was a different man just like Moses, David, and Saul after their own experiences with God.

Many pastors and other congregations came to enjoy our services. I believe people are hungry for the supernatural.

They want to encounter the living powerful God they read about in the Word. This generation, like Gideon, is asking:

> *...Where are all (God's) wonders that our ancestors told us about when they said, "Did not the Lord bring us up out of Egypt?" But now the Lord has abandoned us and given us into the hand of Midian.*
>
> Judges 6:13 NIV

In one service, the speaker came to the platform prepared to preach, but when he asked everyone to join hands to pray before he began his message, the whole twenty-member choir fell under the power of God at the same time! Pastors from other churches literally ran to the altar area to meet with a powerful God after that happened!

I realize that when I discuss these types of experiences, many of my readers may want to question or criticize these events. I was condemned and doubted when I first visited the revival in Florida. I actually had family members who did not want to have anything to do with me after I attended this revival. There has always been a great controversy around mighty moves of God. People are often skeptical of things that they do not understand. In some cases, people are judgmental and in total opposition to the unfamiliar. Skepticism exist because while God moves in a mighty way in one place, He may not move in the same way in another and we question the seemingly inconsistencies. Jesus did many miracles outside His home country. But the scriptures recorded that when He came to His own, He was only able to do a few miracles. The truth is, the attitude and faith of the people determine how much God can do or reveal. Just because we may lack a personal experience of God's presence does not mean that He has changed. He is the same yesterday, today, and forever (Hebrews 13:8). If we seek Him, we will find Him. If you are one of those individuals who questions these experiences, I sincerely hope you will continue with me through this journey with an open mind. Remember, with God all things are possible.

I do understand and encourage caution in discerning spirits, because unfortunately there is always a counterfeit for the real. The enemy uses this very tactic to attempt to stop all moves of God. However, in your caution, make sure you realize that there was no precedent for Moses' burning bush, or for Saul's bright light on a road to Damascus, but that does not make these events any less real.

Our church continued on that path of having special services along with our normal weekly services and we saw God do amazing things. No two meetings were ever the same as we continued on the journey. Along the way, God began to give me different kinds of revelations. Sometimes they would come in a corporate setting, but very often revelations came when I was alone. Sometimes He would just help me to see things in the Bible I had never seen before, or at other times, it would be verbal communication with my spirit. There was also an increase in spiritual dreams at night, and visions or what I call a visual picture that the Lord would paint for me in my mind while I was awake. I have tried to be faithful to record all of those revelations in my journals over the years because I quickly learned that it is not easy to remember the details for long. I am often amazed at the things that I have documented over the years when I review them later.

I want to share one of those moments as I close this leg of the journey. It was a Saturday morning and I was up early before my husband awoke. I went straight to my office where I began a Bible study. I was in the book of Hebrews and I began to see words literally jumping off the pages. I skipped through about six chapters where this happened and the connecting phrases I saw helped me to get a glimpse of how Jesus literally made a bridge for us that brings access between earth and the kingdom of heaven. It is difficult to explain and I have tried to go back to this passage and see what I saw that morning again, but have been unsuccessful.

During this time of revelation, I felt compelled by the Holy Spirit that I needed to go over to my church. I quickly got dressed and drove across town. As I used my key to enter the empty building, I immediately sensed the presence of God in a very tangible way as I heard the words to the song, *How We Need the River* (McAlmon, 2005).

Tammy Davis, our former pastor's wife was in charge of worship at our church. She played the piano beautifully and knew how to flow from song to song in a way that ushered in the presence of God. One of the things that she initiated at our church was to have worship music playing in the sanctuary 24 hours a day. She knew how important it was to create an atmosphere of worship as a place of habitation for the presence of God. I am happy to say we continue this pattern even today.

I pressed repeat on the CD player so the same song would continue, and I began to walk back and forth across the front of our sanctuary as the words to that song played over and over.

> *Lord, I thirst for You*
> *There is no one else who satisfies*
> *My soul longs for You*
> *Like the deer panting for the water*
> *Now I wait for you*
> *Take me to Your courts of glory*
> *Fall upon me Lord*

Give me strength to help me stand
In this dry and weary land
How we need the river
How we need the rain
Living water flow to us again we pray
Shower down Your glory
Shower down Your grace
Let Your holy presence fill this place
Let Your holy presence fill this place
        -Reprinted with permission from Terry McAlmon

(Scripture reading during music: Ezekiel 47:6;8-9)

He said to me, "Son of man, have you seen this?" Then
he brought me and returned me to the bank of the river.
Then he said to me: "This water flows toward the eastern
region, goes down into the valley, and enters the sea.
When it reaches the sea, its waters are healed. And it
shall be that every living thing that moves, wherever the
rivers go, will live."

Deep calls unto deep
Lord we seek to know Your glory
For there is only You
And our hearts cry Abba Father
Now Lord Jesus come
May your love and grace restore us
Breathe upon us Lord
Let Your mercies be brand new
Let the whole world worship You
Jesus free us to worship in spirit and truth
Heal us reveal to us your power.
How we need the river

How we need the rain
Living water flow to us again we pray
Shower down Your glory
Shower down Your grace
Let Your holy presence fill this place
Let Your holy presence fill this place
-Reprinted with permission from Terry McAlmon

I began to declare in prayer that our church was a place for His glory to inhabit. This was the moment that I had a vivid picture painted in my mind by the Lord. I saw the glory of God in the church as a golden light that permeated the whole place and shone out of the windows like a beam. We have large floor-to-ceiling windows and much like the natural sun shines through those windows, I saw His glory beam shining out through the windows. I could view cars driving by and on seeing the light, they would stop and the occupants come inside. As these individuals walked into the glory, they were instantly changed from spectators to participators. Their disease and sin could not stay in this atmosphere. When they came in, those bondages, cancers and tumors just fell off! It was a picture of reckless worship because the glory made everyone aware of the awe of God's power. There was no coaxing; it was a slice of heaven on earth. Our church became a beacon or a type of lighthouse that set a precedent for others to follow as it spreads from region to region.

The next morning, during our normal weekly service, I was on the platform with our worship team, and looking out over the congregation, I began to see an analogy of the experience I had the previous day compared to the storm that had just happened in the south. When Hurricane Katrina came, people did not take a nonchalant approach saying, "I do not think I will participate in this one." When the storm's wind and rain poured in, those in the path were no longer spectators; they were participators! They were experiencing it whether they wanted to or not.

Another interesting comparison that I saw was about the spectators. The news coverage and the victims being evacuated from the area quickly morphed those who began as only spectators into participators. Those individuals impacted by Hurricane Katrina will never be the same. Regardless of how much time passes, their lives have been marked by this event. This was such a great comparison to what I had seen the previous day at the church. People who are impacted by the wind of God's glory are forever transformed. Like Katrina, it is a force that must be recognized, and it cannot be ignored. Prior to the transformation, we try to fit Him into our lives, but after this kind of revelation encounter, we will learn to fit our lives into Him. I believe this is what God wants for His body throughout the world.

So as we come to the close of this leg of the journey, discussing a major storm in the history of our country, we are reminded that if we travel long enough we will realize that it is not always sunny skies and straight roads. It is inevitable that we will eventually travel through some storms, but it is necessary in taking us to our divinely-appointed destinations.

Chapter 3

STORM WARNINGS

Some of the worst storms I have experienced have actually been on a lake, and not in my car. In my elementary years, my family enjoyed camping at the lake. I was my dad's fishing buddy when we were on those trips. There was one particular lake that had a history of bad storms. I guess it had something to do with the landscape and the direction the wind typically came in. It seemed that even on a beautiful day, a horrific storm could blow in without warning.

One morning while my dad and I were fishing, one of those storms unexpectedly came up. My dad knew I was a strong swimmer, but he was so frightened that he handed me a lifejacket and made me put it on. We were in a small boat with stick steering in the front seat. I remember vividly his stern voice, "I will drive along the bank and if we turn over, do not look back, just swim to the bank!" I had never seen my dad this concerned on a lake before.

The rain felt like needles as it penetrated my skin. I hung on for dear life as we went over wave after wave thinking the water was going to come into the boat. Then we came along a shore where there was a houseboat. The men on this boat saw us and waved us over. We were able to bank safely to wait out the storm.

I remember getting inside the shelter of that boat, and feeling so relieved even though I was shivering from fear and being wet and cold.

Regardless of those experiences, my love of the lake and fishing continued into my adult life and my husband was thrilled that he married someone with this passion. We too had many opportunities to weather storms on the lake through the years. One particular storm stands out above all the rest, because God gave me a wonderful message from the events of that day. He really does speak from the storms.

Our children had reached an age where they did not particularly want to get up early and go fishing with their parents. We had decided that they were old enough and that it would be safe to allow them to stay in the locked camper alone on the campground. My husband and I traveled up the lake about thirteen miles to the location where we planned to fish. We had not been there long when suddenly we began to see lightning. Even though we moved quickly to get our poles put away, we did not get the task completed before the wind and rain began to toss us back and forth.

We took off across the lake as fast as we safely could to get back to our children. I was so concerned because this was the first time we had left them alone, and my daughter was very fearful during storms. After about one mile of travel, the alarm on the motor began to sound. Usually this meant that the fuel filter had clogged. We knew we could not risk continuing to drive with it making that sound or the motor might be significantly damaged. My husband stopped the boat and took the cover off the motor. The waves were so high that the water was splashing into the boat. He removed the filter to clean it and a big wave came over at that time causing him to drop the gasket covering the filter into the lake. We were stranded and worried about our children.

The sweats that I wore to keep me warm on that summer morning going across the lake were now soaked, cold, and heavy. I found myself feeling as vulnerable as I did in my younger years with my dad in the storm we survived.

We were floating helplessly across the water toward a rock bluff. Lightning was all around us. I was praying desperately for God to intervene, and for my children to be safe. My husband was frantically trying to come up with a temporary solution so we could start the motor.

As we eventually floated over to the rock wall, I was sitting on the side of the boat to prepare to kick us away as the waves pushed us toward it. I did not want our boat to be damaged by crashing into it. I kicked us away once and then we just began to float along the side of it. While I was sitting on the side of the boat, I looked down and saw a ledge that came out significantly right below the surface of the water. It was as if God just hid us in the cleft of that rock! I was able to step out of the boat onto that ledge in ankle deep water, even though this part of the lake was well over one hundred feet deep. I held the boat steady while my husband cut cardboard to form a temporary gasket for the fuel filter.

By the time he had successfully completed this task, the storm began to subside. We headed down the lake for our children. When we arrived, they were still asleep and had not been aware that there was a storm.

While both of the storms I just described seemed to come unexpectedly, I am sure if access to the internet were available on phones as we have today, we would have known there was a forecast of those storms. Storms can be predicted, they just cannot be prevented. There was ample warning and prediction that Hurricane Katrina was coming. However, there was nothing that could be done to prevent the devastation the storm brought and no one knew for sure how much damage it would do.

Jesus tried to prepare His disciples for storms. He was the great teacher and when His students failed their first test, He allowed them to take it again. He wanted them to learn to practice faith and not to doubt, even and especially in the midst of storms. Here was the first test.

> *And after He got into the boat, His disciples followed Him. And suddenly, behold, there arose a violent storm on the sea, so that the boat was being covered up by the waves; but He was sleeping. And they went and awakened Him, saying, "Lord, rescue and preserve us! We are perishing!" And He said to them, "Why are you timid and afraid, O you of little faith?" Then He got up and rebuked the winds and the sea, and there was a great and wonderful calm (a perfect peaceableness). And the men were stunned with bewildered wonder and marveled, saying, "What kind of Man is this, that even the winds and the sea obey Him!"*
>
> Matthew 8:23-27 AMP

Six chapters later, we see the second test.

> *Then He directed the disciples to get into the boat and go before Him to the other side, while He sent away the crowds. And after He had dismissed the multitudes, He went up into the hills by Himself to pray. When it was evening, He was still there alone. But the boat was by this time out on the sea, many furlongs [a furlong is one-eighth of a mile] distant from the land, beaten and tossed by the waves, for the wind was against them. And in the*

Rhonda Barnes

fourth watch [between 3:00 — 6:00 a.m.] of the night,
Jesus came to them, walking on the sea. And when the
disciples saw Him walking on the sea, they were terrified
and said, "It is a ghost!" And they screamed out with
fright. But instantly He spoke to them, saying, "Take
courage! I AM! Stop being afraid!" And Peter answered
Him, "Lord, if it is You, command me to come to You on
the water." He said, "Come!" So Peter got out of the boat
and walked on the water, and he came toward Jesus.
But when he perceived and felt the strong wind, he was
frightened, and as he began to sink, he cried out, "Lord,
save me" [from death]! Instantly Jesus reached out His
hand and caught and held him, saying to him, "O you of
little faith, why did you doubt?" And when they got into
the boat, the wind ceased. And those in the boat knelt and
worshiped Him, saying, "Truly You are the Son of God!"

Matthew 14:22-33 AMP

There are many important lessons on how to survive the storms of life in these passages. One critical lesson is that we must realize that He is with us in the storms, and He will never forsake us. He promised that He would always be with us, no matter what we are going through. The disciples experienced this literally in one instance with Jesus actually being on the boat with them, and another when He was walking towards them. Jesus allowed the disciples to experience the first test with Him literally by their side. In the second test, Jesus directed them to go without Him, but He was not far from them. Not only was he seemingly absent during the first part of the storm, He did not come to their assistance until the fourth watch of the night. However, in both situations, He was teaching them to have faith and not doubt that He was with them.

I have heard people say that sometimes Jesus calms the storm, and sometimes He calms His children in the midst of the storm. When Jesus calmed both of these storms, the disciples were amazed by His power. The solution seemed as sudden as the storm. Unfortunately, this is not always the case. Often the aftermath of a storm is more difficult than the storm itself. For example, we do not see the effects of flooding, power outages, and destruction of property until after a hurricane is over. The damage can last a very long time and the recovery can be even longer and very costly.

In the past, our congregation had experienced a great storm, and the aftermath of that storm continues for many even now over seven years later at the time of this being written. We were experiencing these amazing times of revival and I had seen this beautiful analogy where the construction of the new highway was representative of the transformation the Lord was doing in our corporate body and in many individuals' lives. Sadly, on Monday, January 8, 2007, the road that represented revival and destiny became the location of a horrible tragedy.

We had an amazing revival service the previous night and we were scheduled to begin service again the next day at 7 p.m. There were buses coming from other churches, and there was much excitement and great anticipation about what the Lord would do.

On my way home from work I was traveling the new highway and was stopped at a roadblock where a highway patrol told me that the road was closed due to a fatal accident. I was sent toward my destination on an alternate route. While I was driving, I was trying to call Tammy, our pastor's wife, to tell her that we needed to reach the churches that were coming by bus to have them take a different route. My calls kept going directly to her voicemail.

A few moments later, I received a call. The fatal accident was Tammy! She and two other amazing ladies from our church had been in a head-on collision with a semi-truck and none of them survived.

About a week later, during a winter storm, I watched from the balcony of our church as over 1,200 people lined up to pay their respects to Tammy and her best friend, who had died with her in the accident. The next day I listened as God gave grace to her husband and children to speak to the group who gathered for the funeral. At the end of the service, I joined our worship team as we went to the platform where she had previously led us, and sang *It is Well with My Soul* (Spafford, 1873).

Truthfully, it was quite a battle over the next days, weeks, and years for me to consistently profess that it was well with my soul. I realized that this tragedy affected everyone differently, but I can only really speak about the impact it had on me personally. Tammy was my cousin and my friend. Coping with the loss of someone special in my life was difficult enough, but in this situation, it was even more complex. She was one of our spiritual leaders who was connected to the divine destiny our corporate body was embarking on. Since she played a critical role in this transformation process that we were in, it was difficult for me to imagine how we were to move forward without her.

There were many days I found myself questioning the Lord as the disciples did in the first storm. They wondered how He could sleep when they were perishing! There were days I could clearly hear His words of comfort in the second storm, *"Take courage! I AM!"* The road to transformation began to feel like a never ending roller coaster ride.

It was very difficult to push past the fact that one of our leaders was absent when we gathered on Saturday nights at our church for prayer. We desperately missed her supply. When we would gather for normal service times, the vacant bench in front of the piano created such a vacuum. It was painful to watch our pastor mustering strength to lead a congregation through such a difficult time, when he too was coping with his own personal loss. I remember many times that the pain was so deep that I felt as if I could not breathe.

Though many days seemed impossible, God's grace sustained us. Not long after the funeral, I wrote in my journal:

> "I do know we are a body in process between the promise and the prophecy. I guess we thought that the transformation process would be through miracles and joy, not through suffering and pain. I see the unity of the people following this tragedy as a force propelling us forward. Now we must begin to navigate this course."

I went on in my journal that day to write a prayer that came from my heart:

> "We need you Holy Spirit to come with healing that only you can bring for our broken hearts. We submit to Your process. Help us to stay 'On Plan' with it in Jesus name! I know in my professional world my performance is evaluated by where I am 'To Plan.' In the business world, I am not satisfied to just meet my performance goals, I want to exceed them! God, let us go above and beyond! Let the people of Grace Community Church be sparked to step up and go above and beyond to exceed Your plan for us! Give us grace – give us strength – give us comfort – give us unction to passionately pursue Your glory with all

our hearts, souls, and strength. Let our grief fuel our passion to see in part here on earth what Tammy and the other women are now experiencing in heaven!"

A few weeks later, I was awakened from a very strange dream. In the dream, I was lying on the ground on the side of a long highway. I was using the guardrail that is often found on the shoulder to literally pull myself inch-by-inch along this long stretch of road, and at the same time thinking to myself that I needed to get up and walk, but I just could not draw enough strength to pull myself to a standing position. The road eventually led through a town, and people were watching me struggle. One man actually whistled at me while driving by! Then there was a break in the guardrail that I was using, and I was trying to figure out how to get enough strength to get to the next section of road where the rail began again. It was at this point in the dream that my alarm clock woke me up.

This dream was a true picture of the section of the road to transformation I was currently traveling. It was inch-by-inch; day by day, putting one foot in front of the other to continue to contend for a destiny, which I knew, was before me in my personal life and in my church.

While many days seemed like the picture my dream painted, there were other days where I found strength to stand up and make more progress. My new theme was, "Just do it sad!" I gave myself permission to feel the sadness, but I could not allow the sadness to make me give up on the journey I was traveling. It was just a detour with some mandated rest stops, but the final destination was still in the plan. Through the process, I often felt stuck between reality and dreams. God was taking me on a journey where my capacity to believe was being enlarged, all the while, testing everything to find the real and the pure. It was a very difficult part of the journey.

Our pastor received a book about comfort for those who grieve. In the back of the book, there was contact information for the author. Pastor reached out to him, and he agreed to come and speak to our church. The one statement this man made that stood out most to me was, "You must choose tragedy or destiny." The choice for me was clear, but the reality of navigating that choice was far more complex.

When I need to hear from God most, He often responds by painting such vivid pictures in my mind that I feel I can literally see what He is saying to me. The beginning of navigating this course happened that way. We had experienced a very bad ice storm in Missouri. A few days after the bad weather, I was traveling between the health care branches I managed. As I was driving and praying, my attention was suddenly drawn from the road in front of me to the trees beside me. These were very tall pine trees along both sides of the road. The ones on the left side of the road bowed over with the weight of the ice. I heard the Lord clearly say:

> "This is a picture of how so many of my people are…
> weighed down by the cares and concerns of this life,
> because they will not give them to Me."

Then my attention immediately went to the other side of the road. The trees on this side had been exposed to sunlight since the storm ended. All of the ice had melted away from these trees and they stood as tall as they normally should. The Lord reminded me of a scripture found in Matthew 11:28-30:

> *"Come to Me, all who are weary and heavy-laden, and*
> *I will give you rest. Take My yoke upon you and learn*
> *from Me, for I am gentle and humble in heart, and YOU*

WILL FIND REST FOR YOUR SOULS. For My
yoke is easy and My burden is light.”

The picture lesson continued. Next, I noticed the trees which had not been able to bear the weight of the ice and had broken and were destroyed. Since I was picturing these trees as God's children, I asked Him in my prayer, “Lord what about the ones which have been destroyed?” Immediately, in my mind, I saw a picture of a huge Victorian house, and I heard Him say, “I can build something new out of them!” Then I saw a vivid picture of a roaring fire and He said, “They do not have to lay on the roadside and rot! They will never be a tree again, but I can make something great out of them, if they will let Me!” It is amazing what God can do with broken pieces, and vessels others may consider in the natural to be worthless and insignificant.

The lesson the Lord was showing me was that we had options after the storm. Some were still weighed down with the cares, the grief, and the mourning. They could cast those cares over on the Lord and He would help all of those concerns to melt away. As a matter of fact, that is exactly what He is asking us to do:

> *Casting the whole of your care [all your anxieties, all your worries, all your concerns, once and for all] on Him, for He cares for you affectionately and cares about you watchfully.*
>
> 1 Peter 5:7 AMP

> *Cast your burden upon the Lord and He will sustain you; He will never allow the righteous to be shaken.*
>
> Psalm 55:22

If the storm seemingly destroyed someone, God was showing me that there was still abundant life available, for nothing is impossible for God. He specializes in making something out of absolutely nothing:

> *Now the earth was formless and void, and darkness was over the surface of the deep, and the Spirit of God was moving over the surface of the waters.*
>
> Genesis 1:2

Look at what God did with an empty and formless world!

He showed me that the trees, which had been broken and cut away from the highway, would never be trees again, but they could be a part of a beautiful home, or a roaring fire to provide much needed warmth. He was teaching me that we could do more than just survive after the storm; we can thrive!

> *The thief comes only to steal and kill and destroy; I came that they may have life, and have it abundantly.*
>
> John 10:10

The scripture highlights the difference in just surviving and thriving. Too many Christians are living life on the wrong side of the comma, especially those who have endured a major storm! Life before the comma in this passage is just surviving, but Jesus died for us so that we can have life more abundantly! This is not just about living. This speaks to growing and experiencing God at greater levels. No storm, no matter the magnitude, can cancel His promises or His provision. For our God is able to do far more exceedingly, abundantly above all we can think, or ask, or even imagine.

During a Sunday service, after the tragedy, our church received the following Word of promise and comfort from the Lord:

> "For I have promised that my grace is sufficient, and ask of you this day; lean on Me, learn of Me, flow with Me. I am not confused, saith the Lord, I know the direction in which to go. As you wait in My presence I will give you direction; I will give you grace. Let Me say again, My grace is sufficient. I know the pain in which you are going through. I have not forsaken you. At times when you have questions, just rest in My presence, and rest assured that I am with you, I am for you. In the coming days, I will give you strength, I will encourage you. In the coming days that you wait upon me, you shall be renewed, in your mind, in your strength. Think not that you are all alone, for I know exactly where you are at, and I have chosen you, and I will heal you, I will fill you. You will know that the greatest hours of My visitation are not behind you, they are in front of you. Let the church rally together in unity. Do not run ahead of Me, saith God, but wait in My presence, for as you wait upon Me, I am coming to you. Even now God has everything under control, saith the Spirit."

Many thought we would not walk in the glory of God's presence the way we once did in our church. Some could not endure the very deep valley that we were forced to walk through; but to those who were determined to overcome – to keep trudging up that steep miry path, pressing and pushing their way out of this wilderness, they began to develop a new stamina to walk and withstand a greater portion of His tangible glory. They learned that His presence was greater than their pressure, and that His blessings were stronger than their battles!

I believe Grace Community Church was selected to be one of the catalysts to usher in the Glory of God on this earth. We have been uniquely qualified to host His presence in an unusual way. The enemy meant to destroy us but instead God gave us hinds' feet.

> *The Lord God is my strength, And He has made my feet like hinds' feet, And makes me walk on my high places....*
> Habakkuk 3:19

Chapter 4

ROAD HAZARDS

Have you ever experienced desperation? I am sure if you have traveled on life's journey long enough you have had opportunities to experience some degree of desperation. If I consider desperation in the sense of extreme intensity, it can actually be a great catalyst to drive one toward their destiny. This is exactly what caused me to study and develop a lesson, which I later called, "The Hazards of Desperation."

If you are comfortable or satisfied where you are, you most likely are not desperate enough to seek transformation. Consider a baby bird; as long as it has a comfortable nest and nourishment brought to it, there is no need to learn to fly. At some point, the momma bird realizes it is time for transformation, and will make the nest less comfortable to cause the baby bird to want to move. Our desperation could result from a desire deep inside us that is yearning for something greater. It could develop from the storms we walk through, an enemy attack, or even a divine plan God puts in place to get us to move beyond where we currently are. A fitting example would be the disciples after Jesus ascended. The purpose of the gospel was that it be spread throughout the world, but the disciples had found a comfort zone in their home cities and towns and would not move beyond its borders. So God allowed the disciples to be persecuted, and this inevitably led to them being scattered. If this was not done, the chances of us receiving the good news of the Kingdom today would have been significantly minimal. The point is, desperation plays a key role in transformation.

Moments of desperation can lead to greater things both good and bad. There are different reasons that propel people into seasons of desperation. For instance, there are many people in our world who do not have adequate food or water. We can read or listen to countless news reports about the desperate acts people will do in search of these life necessities. There are many references in Scripture of severe famines and the drastic measures that resulted from no food. In some cases, people resorted to eating dove's dung or even worse: their own children! (See 2 Kings 7:24-19).

Another issue that causes desperation is sickness and disease. One of the best examples of this phenomenon found in the Bible is one we often refer to as the "woman with the issue of blood."

> *A woman who had had a hemorrhage for twelve years, and had endured much at the hands of many physicians, and had spent all that she had and was not helped at all, but rather had grown worse — after hearing about Jesus, she came up in the crowd behind Him and touched His cloak. For she thought, "If I just touch His garments, I will get well." Immediately the flow of her blood was dried up; and she felt in her body that she was healed of her affliction. Immediately Jesus, perceiving in Himself that the power proceeding from Him had gone forth, turned around in the crowd and said, "Who touched My*

garments?" And His disciples said to Him, "You see the
crowd pressing in on You, and You say, 'Who touched
Me?'" And He looked around to see the woman who had
done this. But the woman fearing and trembling, aware
of what had happened to her, came and fell down before
Him and told Him the whole truth. And He said to her,
"Daughter, your faith has made you well; go in peace and
be healed of your affliction."

Mark 5:25-34

What a picture of desperation! She suffered greatly; she had spent everything she owned, and she had no additional options, until she heard about Jesus. In essence, Jesus was her only hope. Twelve years is a very long time to carry this type of burden. I am sure her physical and emotional strength was depleted. Perhaps she was also in pain. Additionally, according to the law, she was ceremonially unclean and should not be in the public limelight. (See Leviticus 15:19-30). This would have created further religious and social restrictions. This paints a picture of the level of desperation this woman was experiencing when she pressed through the crowd to reach for His garment. Her desperation drove her through crowds, scorn and public scrutiny to achieve her goal.

The blind man, Bartimaeus, like this woman, showed great desire to reach Jesus. He was also desperate for the Healer to intervene in his situation, despite the attempts of those around him, who could see, trying to shut him up.

As Jesus was approaching Jericho, a blind man was sitting
by the road begging. Now hearing a crowd going by, he
began to inquire what this was. They told him that Jesus
of Nazareth was passing by. And he called out, saying,
"Jesus, Son of David, have mercy on me!" Those who

led the way were sternly telling him to be quiet; but he kept crying out all the more, "Son of David, have mercy on me!" And Jesus stopped and commanded that he be brought to Him; and when he came near, He questioned him, "What do you want Me to do for you?" And he said, "Lord, I want to regain my sight!" And Jesus said to him, "Receive your sight; your faith has made you well." Immediately he regained his sight and began following Him, glorifying God; and when all the people saw it, they gave praise to God.

Luke 18:35-43

I love this man! He did not care what others thought or what they said, he was a desperate man. When he realized the uproar of the crowd was a result of Jesus coming near, he was determined to take action. He cried out with all his might, "Jesus, Son of David, have mercy on me!" He was persistent. When he was told to be quiet, his response was to cry even louder, "Jesus, Son of David, have mercy on me!" You see, those around you may never be able to relate to your level of desperation when it comes to seeking God's face. But when you know what you want from God, and you know that only He can provide that very thing – nothing will stand in your way.

I share these examples of desperation because most of us understand the dire need for food, healing, and sight. However, my goal is to encourage this same intense desire for a personal relationship with your Lord and Savior, and that His plans and purposes are fully accomplished in your life. Sadly, too many Christians have become satisfied with the status quo. Many are content to hear what God is speaking to others and never seek to hear His voice themselves. This mindset is similar to the Children of Israel who preferred to hear from Moses than God himself. But God desires a

Rhonda Barnes

personal and intimate relationship with each of us. He wants every one of His sheep to personally know His voice.

God gave me a Word about this during a Wednesday night Bible study and prayer time. We had been experiencing constant rain during the previous week and many places were suffering great damage from flooding. During our service, our pastor asked us to just bow our heads and seek the Lord while the song, *My Soul Longs for You* (Jesus Culture, 2010) played. One line of that song states, "I believe You will come like the rain." As I listened to the words play, the Lord spoke the following revelation to me, and I shared it with my Church.

> *Just as the natural rain has fallen to the degree that the ground is so totally saturated that there is an overflow to the point of flooding, so it is in the Spirit. I am beginning to pour out the rain of My Spirit on a dry and thirsty land. As My people become saturated with My presence, there will begin to be an overflow from the abundance of rain that will flood to the low places. You may say, "But what about the destruction that the flooding is causing?" The flood of My Spirit will break through the walls and barriers of tradition and man's limits. There will be destruction of the walls man's plans have created, and the rain of My Spirit will flow to places it has not gone to before. It will break through the walls of bondage and addiction, and the floodwaters will carry you forward. When you say, "We are moving forward," you say it and do not really believe it; or do not really mean it, or possibly do not understand it. You have taken your theory of revival or awakening and have packaged it so beautifully and even tied it up with a big bow to try to make it "fit" in your current way of life; but when the flood of My presence really comes, it will wash away*

all of your theories. It will wash away all you plans, and programs, and all the debris that goes with it. It will rearrange your lives to the degree that your priorities will line up with My priorities. You will be forced to evacuate from the places of comfort, and become focused on necessity. The price to your flesh will be very high, but your Spirit man will rise to a new high, to flood-stage level. During a time of flooding, people are forced to move to higher ground. The flood of My Spirit will move you to a higher place, to a new level of revelation, to a new level of understanding, to a higher level of function and flow in the gifts of My Spirit; and you will flow to places you do not know. Again I say, "Go in the flow you do not know; yield to the flow you cannot control!"

This Word is about desperation! First, it is a promise from the Lord to pour out His Spirit on those who are desperately hungry and thirsty for His presence. Similar to the way Bartimaeus cried out with intense desire because he did not want Jesus to pass him by, there is a remnant in the Body of Christ who are desperate for God to pour out His Spirit in such a way that they are crying out, "Jesus, Son of David, have mercy on us!"

These are so passionate for His presence that they are willing to "evacuate from their place of comfort and move to a higher place." They are willing to pay the price of sacrificing their flesh. What does that mean? It is different for each of us. It may mean we replace time we spend watching television, enjoying social media, or other leisure interests, with activities that promote spiritual growth. It may require that we step out of our own unique comfort zones. For some, that might involve sharing their faith at work. Perhaps some need to step out into ministry opportunities. Maybe others just need to stop being "undercover" Christians. There is a rule of thumb here worthy of consideration, and that is if we keep doing the same things, we will always yield the same results.

The Lord has made us a promise that if we are willing to abandon our plans, He will give us the anointing and the unction from the gifts of the Holy Spirit to flow into realms and places that in our own plans we can never go. There is a song sung by Hillsong (2011) called *Believe* which describes this concept I am expressing so well. It depicts people who focus more on religion than on a personal relationship with their Savior. These individuals often live differently on Sunday than they do the remainder of the week, and their corporate church gathering is more of a ritual for them than a worship experience. Desperate people are not satisfied with those limits. Desperate people express what this song says: *I'm not satisfied to have the form but not the power.*

These lyrics describe a person who is desperate for God's best. When my trio sang this song, I had difficulty getting through the song, because I feel so passionately about the message. So many Christians have reduced their relationship with Jesus to simply attending a weekly service, and they walk away and never think about their Redeemer again until the next week's gathering! Too many are satisfied reciting the miracles from revival services experienced long ago, instead of building on those encounters and pursuing new and greater ones. I am not interested in a form without power. Jesus told the disciples they would receive power when the Holy Spirit came (See Acts 1). He expected that they would do greater things than He had done while He was on the earth.

> *Truly, truly, I say to you, he who believes in Me, the works that I do, he will do also; and greater works than these he will do; because I go to the Father. Whatever you*

ask in My name, that will I do, so that the Father may be glorified in the Son. If you ask Me anything in My name, I will do it.

John 14:12-14

We cannot be content living in a reality that opposes the Word of God. If Jesus said it, then consider it a fact. The absence of the experience does not negate the truth of what was said. We need to pursue it until it becomes a reality. The very practice of faith speaks to this concept. We need to speak things that are not as if they were. We need to believe what the Word of God says, and not fall victims to the mindset of what our present reality seemingly is. When we get to that place, then it must be pursued. Bartimaeus wanted the healing that Jesus could provide. He was not satisfied continuing life without sight. The men around him told him to be quiet, but after his persistence, Jesus responded to his desperate cry. Like Bartimaeus, I have not seen everything I want to see yet, and that makes me desperate!

Up to this point, I have been describing a type of desperation associated with intense desire, but there is another form of desperation that we must consider. This kind of desperation is connected to hopelessness. Desperation can be a positive force that propels momentum, or it can be a negative force, which encourages defeat. While traveling on the road to transformation, there are many destructive hazards of desperation that would encourage us to detour from the best course.

DISAPPOINTMENT

Life is permeated with disappointments, but none can penetrate deeper than those connected with our faith.

Rhonda Barnes

Disappointment and expectation are closely linked. If we allow ourselves to presume a certain outcome, we open a door for disappointment when the result varies from our expectation.

Many people who have been so desperate for a move of God, so desperate for a promise to be fulfilled, or those who have contended for the miraculous, can find themselves feeling disappointed when the answer does not seem to come. Disappointment is a weapon that the enemy loves to use against God's children. If not dealt with, it will progress to a more serious hazard of desperation, which is disillusionment.

Disillusionment

Just as disappointment is closely linked to expectation, I believe disillusionment is connected to doubt. Disillusionment can be a very dangerous circumstance. When we entertain this hazard, we begin to question the real from the lie. The enemy of our soul is the "father of lies" and there is no truth in him (John 8:44). One of his greatest weapons is convincing Christians that what they believe about God is false, or that His promises are not true. The enemy causes us to question God, thereby casting doubt on what He says in His Word. If the enemy is unable to infuse unbelief, he will attempt to make us believe y=we missed God's plan, timing, or direction. The Bible is clear about the hazards associated with doubt.

> But if any of you lacks wisdom, let him ask of God, who gives to all generously and without reproach, and it will be given to him. But he must ask in faith without any doubting, for the one who doubts is like the surf of the sea, driven and tossed by the wind. For that man ought not to

*expect that he will receive anything from the Lord, being
a double-minded man, unstable in all his ways.*

James 1:5-8

The road to transformation is a process. Some parts of the journey can feel very lengthy. During these times of waiting, it is easy to entertain disappointment because of unmet expectations. Then after further delay, there is a progression from this state to doubt and disillusionment. Consider the story of Lazarus as an example.

Jesus loved this family. When Mary sent word to Jesus that her brother was sick, I suspect she had an expectation that He would come to heal him. She had witnessed many of the miracles Jesus had performed. Surely, He would come when they so desperately needed him. When Jesus delayed His coming, and Lazarus continued to grow worse, I believe there was a prime opportunity for disappointment to overtake Mary. As his sickness progressed to death, the opening for disillusionment was great. The Bible says that when the family heard that Jesus was coming, Martha went to meet him, but Mary stayed at the house. Knowing how much Mary loved Jesus, I have to wonder if this behavior shows her disillusionment.

Martha therefore, when she heard that Jesus was coming, went to meet Him, but Mary stayed at the house. Martha then said to Jesus, "Lord, if You had been here, my brother would not have died. Even now I know that whatever You ask of God, God will give You." Jesus said to her, "Your brother will rise again." Martha said to Him, "I know that he will rise again in the resurrection on the last day." Jesus said to her, "I am the resurrection and the life; he who believes in Me will live even if he dies,

Rhonda Barnes

and everyone who lives and believes in Me will never die. Do you believe this?" She said to Him, "Yes, Lord; I have believed that You are the Christ, the Son of God, even He who comes into the world." When she had said this, she went away and called Mary her sister, saying secretly, "The Teacher is here and is calling for you." And when she heard it, she got up quickly and was coming to Him. Now Jesus had not yet come into the village, but was still in the place where Martha met Him. Then the Jews who were with her in the house, and consoling her, when they saw that Mary got up quickly and went out, they followed her, supposing that she was going to the tomb to weep there. Therefore, when Mary came where Jesus was, she saw Him, and fell at His feet, saying to Him, "Lord, if You had been here my brother would not have died." When Jesus therefore saw her weeping, and the Jews who came with her also weeping, He was deeply moved in spirit and was troubled, and said, "Where have you laid him?" They said to Him, "Lord, come and see." Jesus wept. So the Jews were saying, "See how He loved him!" But some of them said, "Could not this man, who opened the eyes of the blind man, have kept this man also from dying?" So Jesus, again being deeply moved within, came to the tomb. Now it was a cave, and a stone was lying against it. Jesus said, "Remove the stone." Martha, the sister of the deceased, said to Him, "Lord, by this time there will be a stench, for he has been dead four days." Jesus said to her, "Did I not say to you that if you believe, you will see the glory of God?" So they removed the stone. Then Jesus raised His eyes, and said, "Father, I thank You that You have heard Me. I knew that You always hear Me; but because of the people standing around I said it, so that they may believe that You sent Me." When He

*had said these things, He cried out with a loud voice,
"Lazarus, come forth." The man who had died came
forth, bound hand and foot with wrappings, and his face
was wrapped around with a cloth. Jesus said to them,
"Unbind him, and let him go."*

John 11:20-44

Notice the response of both Martha and Mary as they
individually addressed Jesus in this passage, "If You had
been here." Have you ever allowed the "ifs" of life's journey
to push you into disillusionment? Have you ever questioned
how a loving God could allow you to face certain events? It
is a natural human tendency to do so. In this scenario, the
Master's intervention turned the whole situation around, but
if disillusionment is not dealt with, it will progress to the final
hazard of desperation.

DISENGAGEMENT

This word can be a military term used to describe the
withdrawal of troops from a war or combat. When we
disengage in a spiritual context, we withdraw from our
place of purpose. It may not be that an individual gives up
their Christianity; it could be that they become weary and
disengage from their passionate pursuit to settle for the status
quo.

Consider this concept a different way. Disengagement
could also be an example of breaking off an engagement to
be married. Even though it has been over 30 years now, I
still vividly remember getting my engagement ring. I did not
want to give it up to have it sized, and when I finally had it
back, I could not stop looking at it. I recall driving with my

hand propped on the top of the steering wheel so I could look at it frequently during travel! When opportunities presented themselves for me to become disappointed or disillusioned with my future spouse, I did not take the engagement ring off, but instead I pressed through the difficult times, and we have a beautiful relationship to show for that commitment today. As believers, we are called *The Bride of Christ*. Our heavenly Bridegroom wants us to be engaged, excited, and relentless in our pursuit of Him.

Elijah was a great example of someone who suffered from the hazards of desperation. He was a passionate man who was desperate for the people to rely on the one true God. He was determined to destroy the false prophets of Baal (See 1 Kings 18). In one instance, he went up against all the prophets of Baal to prove who is the one, true living God is. Baal never responded to their call, but when Elijah prayed, fire fell from heaven and consumed his sacrifice and he enjoyed a great victory. When the power of God came on him, he even outran a chariot! Unfortunately, shortly after what was probably one of his greatest triumphs, he plunged deep into the hazards of his desperate pursuit.

> Now Ahab told Jezebel all that Elijah had done, and how he had killed all the prophets with the sword. Then Jezebel sent a messenger to Elijah, saying, "So may the gods do to me and even more, if I do not make your life as the life of one of them by tomorrow about this time." And he was afraid and arose and ran for his life and came to Beersheba, which belongs to Judah, and left his servant there. But he himself went a day's journey into the wilderness, and came and sat down under a juniper tree; and he requested for himself that he might die, and

said, "It is enough; now, O Lord, take my life, for I am
not better than my fathers."

1 Kings 19:1-4

How did this strong man of faith, who had just prayed fire down from heaven, allow one woman's threat to destroy his momentum? I assume he faced great disappointment when he received the warning. I can imagine the disillusionment as he ran for his life. Ultimately, he is found under a juniper tree, totally disengaged from his purpose, and requesting to die!

It is easy to be critical of Elijah's seeming weakness. However, the reality is, most of us traveling a road to transformation can easily relate to him. The good news is that our Lord loves us too much to leave us when we are in this state. He understands that sometimes our journey does offer great opportunity for disappointment and disillusionment. He does not give up on us even when we disengage and quit on Him!

God dealt with the disappointed and disillusioned Elijah in an understanding and compassionate way. He allowed the exhausted Elijah to sleep, He nourished him with food, He visited him with an awe-inspiring revelation of His power and presence, and He provided him with additional direction to set him back on track.

Then he came there to a cave and lodged there; and
behold, the word of the Lord came to him, and He said to
him, "What are you doing here, Elijah?" He said, "I have
been very zealous for the Lord, the God of hosts; for the
sons of Israel have forsaken Your covenant, torn down
Your altars and killed Your prophets with the sword. And
I alone am left; and they seek my life, to take it away."
So He said, "Go forth and stand on the mountain before

the Lord." And behold, the Lord was passing by! And a great and strong wind was rending the mountains and breaking in pieces the rocks before the Lord; but the Lord was not in the wind. And after the wind an earthquake, but the Lord was not in the earthquake. After the earthquake a fire, but the Lord was not in the fire; and after the fire a sound of a gentle blowing. When Elijah heard it, he wrapped his face in his mantle and went out and stood in the entrance of the cave. And behold, a voice came to him and said, "What are you doing here, Elijah?" Then he said, "I have been very zealous for the Lord, the God of hosts; for the sons of Israel have forsaken Your covenant, torn down Your altars and killed Your prophets with the sword. And I alone am left; and they seek my life, to take it away."

1 Kings 19:9-14

Let me emphasize two important points about this text. First, notice what the voice of the Lord said to Elijah twice. "What are you doing here, Elijah?" Is it possible He was asking Elijah, "Why have you disengaged?" Secondly, if we consider his response to the Lord, "I am very zealous for the Lord…" or perhaps we could assume he is speaking from the perspective of being very desperate for the Lord. Through his desperation and faithful service to the Lord, he finds himself in a place he should not be. Thankfully, God in His mercy, expressed His amazing power and presence to renew Elijah's focus, and he left from that place to fulfill the remaining call on his life.

One of the many lessons I have learned on the road to transformation is that it is always darkest right before dawn. Your greatest battle will often come prior to the ultimate breakthrough. Everything can change in just a moment, just as it did for Elijah in that cave.

Chapter 5

ROUTINE TRAFFIC STOP

Suppose while you are traveling along the road we have been discussing, you notice lights flashing in your rearview mirror along with the sound of a siren warning you to pull over. When you are safely on the shoulder of the road, a friendly highway patrol approaches, and politely informs you that this is a simple routine traffic stop to assure you have a valid license, registration, and insurance card. After a few moments of research, the officer returns with a stern look on his face. He states, "Ma'am, I am going to need you to come with me. It appears you have been a victim of identity theft!"

These are the exact words I heard the Holy Spirit speak to me while I was attending a conference in Dallas, Texas. I had just participated in an amazing worship service, and was about to settle in to listen to a sermon by a minister who had unbelievable revelation but much to my surprise, the revelation did not come as I expected.

The best way I can describe the encounter is comparing it to a scene in a movie I once watched. A pitcher was about to deliver a critical throw that could lead to an important win. As he stood on the mound, the crowd roared loudly, but then the sound in the movie faded and all that could be heard was the pitcher's breathing as he entered into the "zone." I experienced a similar phenomenon during this service. It was as if suddenly someone began to turn the volume down on the minister's microphone and his voice began to fade to the background. Then I heard the Holy Spirit speak these words, "You have been a victim of identity theft!"

At that moment I turned my phone on audio record to tape the message that was being preached because I was about to hear a very different message. It was not words I had not heard before or truths that were new to me, but they were revealed to me in a different way and the impact was substantial.

Two days later, I returned home from Dallas. When I went through the mail that was sitting on the counter, I came across an envelope from a company that I had never heard of before. The return address read, "LifeLock, Relentlessly Protecting Your Identity." In red letters across the side of the envelope was written, "Identity theft? I don't think that'll happen to me." I opened the envelope, and began reading the letter,

> "Most of us think we're the last person that would ever have their identity stolen...Dear Rhonda Barnes, With over 12.6 million Americans having fallen victim to identity theft in 2012 alone, it's all too common to hear stories of how this crime has had a lasting and detrimental impact on people's lives. We just don't think it can happen to us..."

My Spirit was leaping inside of me with the confirmation the Holy Spirit had just provided. I had just heard the words,

"Rhonda, you have been a victim of identity theft" two days prior to receiving this letter.

During the revelation, the first point that the Holy Spirit made to me was that I had been a victim. What is a victim? *Merriam-Webster's Collegiate Dictionary* (2005) defines it as, "One who is subjected to oppression, hardship, or mistreatment. Somebody who is tricked or exploited. To fall victim to somebody or something, to be effected, harmed, or deceived by somebody or something."

I think most understand the concept of a victim, but what really stood out to me was the fact that a victim is just that, a victim. When it comes to being a victim of identity theft, the person did not ask to be a target; they did not choose to be a prey, but someone recognized the value that this person has and made them a target. This is why so many are caught off guard when it happens and often do not even recognize that it has happened for a very long time.

If you consider this concept from a spiritual perspective, a person may be doing all the right things, serving God to the best of his ability, actively involved in the local body or even in a personal ministry. He may be studying the Word and praying, but then one day there is a realization that his identity has been stolen.

A very familiar scripture found in John 10:10 states, "The thief comes only to steal and kill and destroy; I came that they may have life, and have it abundantly." The thief comes to steal, kill, and destroy, because what we have is worth stealing! The thief knows the value of what we possess in our mortal bodies, and is determined to destroy it.

In a recent sermon, my pastor said, "The more powerful your purpose and destiny, the more you will find yourself under enemy attack." Someone who has nothing to steal is most likely not going to find themselves a victim of theft.

Usually when we think of identity theft in the natural, we associate it with someone stealing our name. This is where it begins. If you ask me what my name is, I can easily tell you my name, I can quote my birth date, I can recite my social security number, where I am from and who my parents are. For the sake of this point, engage your imagination for just a moment and pretend that you are a soldier and you have been captured in enemy territory.

You were trained to withstand all kinds of enemy force to protect your military secrets. However, day after day you are beaten, deprived of sleep, and bombarded with lies continuously. After a while, you discover that you do not even know who you are anymore. Does that sound familiar? We have an enemy who knows what tactics to use, according to our own individual weaknesses, to cause us to question who we are in Christ. Satan knows well who we are; he is just doing everything in his power to keep us from discovering who we are. He knows that if we have that revelation, he will forever be defeated!

There are many scriptures which describe our Christian identity, but my favorite is found in Ephesians in the Amplified Bible.

> *Even as [in His love] He chose us [actually picked us out for Himself as His own] in Christ before the foundation of the world, that we should be holy (consecrated and set apart for Him) and blameless in His sight, even above reproach, before Him in love. For He foreordained us (destined us, planned in love for us) to be adopted (revealed) as His own children through Jesus Christ, in accordance with the purpose of His will [because it pleased Him and was His kind intent]...*

Rhonda Barnes

In Him we also were made [God's] heritage (portion) and we obtained an inheritance; for we had been foreordained (chosen and appointed beforehand) in accordance with His purpose, Who works out everything in agreement with the counsel and design of His [own] will, So that we who first hoped in Christ [who first put our confidence in Him have been destined and appointed to] live for the praise of His glory! In Him you also who have heard the Word of Truth, the glad tidings (Gospel) of your salvation, and have believed in and adhered to and relied on Him, were stamped with the seal of the long-promised Holy Spirit. That [Spirit] is the guarantee of our inheritance [the firstfruits, the pledge and foretaste, the down payment on our heritage], in anticipation of its full redemption and our acquiring [complete] possession of it — to the praise of His glory…

By having the eyes of your heart flooded with light, so that you can know and understand the hope to which He has called you, and how rich is His glorious inheritance in the saints (His set-apart ones), And [so that you can know and understand] what is the immeasurable and unlimited and surpassing greatness of His power in and for us who believe, as demonstrated in the working of His mighty strength, Which He exerted in Christ when He raised Him from the dead and seated Him at His [own] right hand in the heavenly [places], Far above all rule and authority and power and dominion and every name that is named [above every title that can be conferred], not only in this age and in this world, but also in the age and the world which are to come. And He has put all things under His feet and has appointed Him the universal and supreme Head of the church [a headship exercised throughout the church]. .

But God — so rich is He in His mercy! Because of and in order to satisfy the great and wonderful and intense love with which He loved us, Even when we were dead (slain) by [our own] shortcomings and trespasses, He made us alive together in fellowship and in union with Christ; [He gave us the very life of Christ Himself, the same new life with which He quickened Him, for] it is by grace (His favor and mercy which you did not deserve) that you are saved (delivered from judgment and made partakers of Christ's salvation). And He raised us up together with Him and made us sit down together [giving us joint seating with Him] in the heavenly sphere [by virtue of our being] in Christ Jesus (the Messiah, the Anointed One).

Ephesians 1:4-5; 11-14; 18-24; 2:4-6 AMP

Wow! This text tells us who are really are in Christ in no uncertain terms. These Words spoken by He who created us affirms our true identity. For us to believe and accept anything contrary to this is to embrace a lie.

As I stated earlier, usually when we think of identity theft in the natural, we associate it with someone stealing our name. However, in the spiritual context of this message, the Holy Spirit revealed to me that the enemy is trying to steal three other parts of our identity. Those are our wealth, our health, and our future. All three are very connected to the overall goal of stealing our identity in Christ. In the process of targeting each of these, Satan has very specific strategies he uses. We have to uncover these tactics and put a halt to them! The scriptures emphasize that we perish for lack of knowledge. The purpose of this book is to elevate you above the shores of ignorance, and place you in a position of power.

It is in knowing that we eventually become who we were meant to be, and ultimately crush the head of the serpent.

WEALTH

When we say the enemy wants to steal your wealth it is true that he wants your finances, but it goes much deeper than that. There are more scriptures in the Bible about money than many of the other topics we teach and preach about today. Why is this? I believe it is because money carries much power. It carries power in society and it carries power in your own life.

The Bible tells us to store up treasures in heaven, for where our treasure is, there our heart will be also (Matt 6:20-21). Far too many Christians are more interested in storing up treasures on earth, and it is this temptation that keeps their focus on material things instead of heavenly things.

There are also many Christians who truly desire to store treasure in heaven, but the reality of the demands that are placed on them to make ends meet in today's society is a constant distraction from heavenly things. Our finances are often directly related to our profession or our job. This is one of the enemy's prime target areas. The pressure, time commitment, and physical and mental strain a job can place on a person can be a heavy burden to bear. While our finances and our profession define our wealth, I feel it is also defined by our time.

Time is the one commodity we never have enough of and once it is gone, we can never get it back. The enemy's strategy is to steal our money and our time. In the end, the circle of chaos that this creates steals our identity.

There are many people in our society today working two jobs for seemingly less pay. It is not that our salaries are not adequate, but the cost of living has increased at a far greater percentage than our increase in salary. Now we spend most of our time making money, but not making enough. The enemy has subtly succeeded in robbing us of both time and money.

Our perception of money and the purpose of money need to change. God has placed in each of us an innate ability to create wealth for His kingdom. He has the ideas that if we execute it well, it can lead to the level of prosperity that He desires for us.

HEALTH

The second thing that the enemy targets in his agenda to steal your identity is your health. Not only does Satan target your physical health, he targets your mental health, your emotional health, and most importantly, your spiritual health.

If there is one thing that will cause you to question your identity, it is a long battle with a physical illness. I do not know why so many Christians are sick, but I do know that Jesus paid the price so we can be healed. I have fought many health issues in my life, and I have been dramatically healed many times. Sometimes healing has come quickly, and sometimes it seemed to take too long. I am convinced that when the enemy has been successful in causing me to lose my identity in Christ, that is when I have been more susceptible to this kind of attack.

The devil does not just target our physical health, he targets our mental health. Some of the symptoms many people suffer from because of this enemy strategy are depression, anxiety, fear, and insomnia. He erodes our mental health with bombarding lies. The Bible tells us that it is his nature and his work to deceive. There is no truth in him. He is the father of lies (John 8:44).

He also seeks to destroy our emotional health. This can come because of relationship challenges, life's disappointments, loss of loved ones, and family disputes. By using some or all of these strategies, the ultimate goal is to destroy our spiritual health.

I feel you can define your spiritual health and well-being by your current personal relationship with the Lord Jesus Christ. Often, we define who we are by what we do, what others believe, or whom we are with; but this is a dangerous error. Do not allow others to determine your identity. Others can reject you, squelch you, try to intimidate you, judge you, and make fun of you; but in the end, man cannot establish your identity. The truth is, your identity has already been established before the foundations of the earth. We have read it in Ephesians 1: *"Even as [in His love] He chose us [actually picked us out for Himself as His own] in Christ before the foundation of the world, that we should be holy (consecrated and set apart for Him) and blameless in His sight, even above reproach, before Him in love."*

Your profession, ministry, or the work you do for God should not define your identity. Too many times we replace intimacy with activity. Your relationship with Jesus establishes your identity and your activity should flow out of that love relationship.

Future

In this grand scheme of identity theft, the enemy has aimed for your name, your wealth, your health, and ultimately he wants to destroy your future. Your future includes your purpose, your passion, and your destiny. Far too many Christians will pass from this life with unseen dreams, misplaced passion and purpose, and unfulfilled destinies. It is no surprise that the greatest wealth in this world lies dormant in our cemeteries, never to be realized, explored and brought to fruition.

Before He formed you in your mother's womb, He knew you. He anointed and appointed you for a specific purpose. In His Master Plan, only you are created with the divine design that will fulfill your unique place. The Bible tells us in Romans 11:29 that the gifts and callings of God are irrevocable! That means they are unchangeable, irreversible, and final! God has not changed His mind! A well-known passage from Jeremiah 29:11-12 says,

> *"For I know the plans that I have for you," declares the Lord, "plans for welfare and not for calamity to give you a future and a hope."*

If the enemy's tactics have caused you to get spiritual amnesia and forget who you are, it is time for you to remember. It is time for you to take back your identity! The first step is the discovery that your identity has been stolen. I am confident that as I have identified some of these tactics, many readers have had an awareness of where they have been vulnerable. You have a unique opportunity right now to turn all that around.

In the natural, when one discovers that they have been a victim of identity theft, they have to get the authorities involved. It is the same concept in the spiritual. Once you discover you have been a victim, it is time to take authority. We read earlier in the book of Ephesians about who we are in Christ, what our inheritance is as a saint, and our authority. Remember Ephesians 1:21?

Far above all rule and authority and power and dominion and every name that is named, not only in this age and in this world, but also in the age and the world which are to come.

We also read in Luke 10:19 ,

Behold, I have given you authority to tread on serpents and scorpions, and over all the power of the enemy, and nothing will injure you.

If we know who we are in Christ, we understand the authority that is available to us through the blood of Jesus. Let me explain it this way. I have authority in my job as a manager over employees. I do not need to display that authority until a situation arises. If an employee begins to behave in a way that is against policies and procedures, I have a choice, as the person in authority, to turn my head and ignore the behavior or use my authority to bring correction to the situation. As a child of God, you have an opportunity to ignore the behavior of the enemy or use the authority you have through Jesus to demand that the activity cease and desist.

You may be reading this and saying, "I already know those scriptures. I already know what is available to me as a joint heir with Christ. I am just not seeing any change!" I am sorry to say, you are still a victim! Taking authority coupled with faith in who God is, and who you are in Him will always yield results.

Faith is the substance of things hoped for, the evidence of things not yet seen (Hebrews 11:1). We can know in our heads what the scripture says. We can use our faith to hope for that promise that we have not yet seen; but there is a moment when that hope, and that head knowledge translates to a

"Word" from God and it becomes a "Revelation" or a heart knowledge that will produce a change.

When this revelation occurs, there is divine disclosure of something that was previously hidden to your heart. When God opens this truth to you, it unlocks what was previously only hoped for. This is what happened to me at Dallas. I knew in my head who I was in Christ, I even continued to quote and pursue those truths, but in reality, I had allowed the storms and the disappointments of the journey to cloud my vision. The Holy Spirit intervened in my situation and gave me a fresh revelation of who I was in Christ and with that restored vision I was able to take back what the enemy had stolen from me. I was able to get back on the road to transformation!

During the six years I taught adult education, I saw this concept repeatedly. Students could memorize and recite a principle to me; but eventually they processed the information and really got it. In the absence of revelation, we will resort back to what we know from past experience and this will result in lack of forward momentum because we are locked up in what used to be.

We began this chapter with a solution to natural identity theft being a company called "Lifelock." I am closing with the spiritual solution to identity theft; the giver of life wants to unlock the things the enemy has locked up!

There are things that the enemy has stolen and locked away from you. He causes you to question who you are, where your place is, and what your purpose is. He has told you it is too late, you are not worthy, you are not qualified, and many more lies. The good news is that the giver of life has the keys to the kingdom, keys to unlock those things that the enemy has stolen and locked away. The revelation of who you are in Christ comes with the authority to take back everything the enemy has stolen and hidden from you. As a matter of fact, Jesus says He will give you the keys to the kingdom:

> *I will give you the keys of the kingdom of heaven, and whatever you bind on earth shall be bound in heaven, and whatever you loose on earth shall be loosed in heaven.*
> Matthew 16:17 ESV

The natural remedy for identity theft is "Lifelock." The spiritual remedy is LIFE UNLOCKED! The giver of life unlocks identity theft, unlocks life in you! He unlocks your name, your wealth, your health! He unlocks your future, your purpose, your passion, and your destiny!

God's economy and laws are very different from man's or this world's economy system. When we consider wealth, God's law says *"Give, and it will be given to you. A good measure, pressed down, shaken together and running over, will be poured into your lap. For with the measure you use, it will be measured to you,"* (Luke 6:38) but man's laws says to save everything and store up treasures here on this earth.

When facing health challenges, men often view the circumstances as impossible, there is nothing else to do. However, God says, *"Nothing is impossible with God!"* (Luke 1:37). When man contemplates the future, he often focuses on our destruction, our failing economy, and our planet that is in trouble. However, God says, *"I know the plans that I have for you...plans for welfare and not for calamity to give you a future and a hope" (Jeremiah 29:11-12).*

Here is the paradox. We live in a human body which is subject to man's laws, but our Spirit man follows God's economy. Therefore, there is always a war between our flesh and our Spirit. In our flesh, we need to process and cope with the realities we face, but, if we want to enjoy God's plan in

God's economy, we have to stretch our faith and suppress our fleshly thinking and align our thoughts with God's thinking.

If you have battled a situation for a long time, it is a normal human process to go through the stages of coping to finally accept that this situation is your new normal. Nevertheless, faith asks us to go against that normal human tendency and hope for what we cannot see. You literally have to push against the tide, even when most people around you allow the flowing tide to take them wherever it desires.

The challenge comes when our human understanding says, "Accept that this is as good as it gets...I can't risk hoping for more because then I have to risk enduring the disappointment all over again if my desires are unfulfilled!" You must remember that during this temptation you are a joint-heir with Jesus seated far above all principalities. Do not let the enemy or life's circumstances lock you into victim mentality! Unlock your destiny.

I imagine that when the Israelites stood at the Red Sea with the Egyptian Army in full pursuit, it seemed to be an impossible situation. Marching around Jericho in silence to get walls to fall down must have seemed impossible. Feeding 5,000 with five loaves of bread and two fishes felt impossible. Having a baby in her nineties had to feel impossible to Sarah! Getting pregnant as a virgin was naturally impossible for Mary.

Your situation may feel impossible, but with God, *"All things are possible to him who believes!"* (Mark 9:23). Unlock your faith! Dare to believe again and stand on the promises God has given you. In this kind of battle, the greatest sustained victory will come when you personally take your own stand!

Just because you have been a victim once does not mean you will not be targeted again! You must learn to take your place daily – sometimes hourly – or even minute-by-minute!

Chapter 6

VIEW FROM THE DAM

If you see a glass with some water in it, would you say it is half-full or half-empty? Both are actually true, but it's your personal perspective which drives your unique response. Similarly, there are pictures available that have two or more distinct images that can be viewed. These are sometimes referred to as perceptual rivalry. One of the best-known versions is a picture of a young woman versus an old lady. Some individuals only see the young woman in the picture, others see only the old, yet many can visualize both. It is related to each person's unique point of view.

Some people tend to see the big picture; others focus on the details. Maybe you have heard it described as the forest and the trees. Some people see the forest but miss the trees; others see the trees and miss the forest. Another way to consider this concept is with vision disturbances. If a person suffers from nearsightedness, she can see close objects clearly, but distance detail is blurry. These compare to those who focus on the trees. Farsightedness is just the opposite. The forest, or distant vision is clear, but the close objects are blurry.

Spiritual perception is critical on the road to transformation. The healthiest perspective is to view the forest and still enjoy the shade of every tree. There are many things that can influence your perspective, but I want to focus on three.

> *Now as they were traveling along, He entered a village; and a woman named Martha welcomed Him into her home. She had a sister called Mary, who was seated at the Lord's feet, listening to His word. But Martha was distracted with all her preparations; and she came up to Him and said, "Lord, do You not care that my sister has left me to do all the serving alone? Then tell her to help me." But the Lord answered and said to her, "Martha, Martha, you are worried and bothered about so many things; but only one thing is necessary, for Mary has chosen the good part, which shall not be taken away from her."*
>
> Luke 10:38-42

The first thing that will affect your perspective is distraction. Many people face these challenges in the activities of their everyday life. This was the case for Martha. She was so distracted with all the work that needed to be done that she was feeling overwhelmed, and she missed what was most important. Mary's point of view was very different from Martha's, and Jesus emphasizes the best insight.

Can you imagine being so busy and distracted that you miss an opportunity to sit at the feet of the greatest teacher ever known? This is exactly how many Christians function. They are too overwhelmed with the cares of life, and too distracted with the business of activities to spend time at the feet of Jesus. If we are to learn from Him, we need to be with Him. It is okay to leave a little dirt on the floor, the dishes piling up, and the laundry basket full if it is the only way to spend time sitting at Jesus feet.

Rhonda Barnes

The next example of a dramatic difference in viewpoint is from the book of Numbers. In this story, Moses sends twelve men to explore the land of Canaan, their future Promised Land. He wanted them to learn about the land, the people, and the crops. However, when the spies returned, there were two very different perspectives.

Thus they told him, and said, "We went in to the land where you sent us; and it certainly does flow with milk and honey, and this is its fruit. Nevertheless, the people who live in the land are strong, and the cities are fortified and very large; and moreover, we saw the descendants of Anak there. Amalek is living in the land of the Negev and the Hittites and the Jebusites and the Amorites are living in the hill country, and the Canaanites are living by the sea and by the side of the Jordan." Then Caleb quieted the people before Moses and said, "We should by all means go up and take possession of it, for we will surely overcome it." But the men who had gone up with him said, "We are not able to go up against the people, for they are too strong for us." So they gave out to the sons of Israel a bad report of the land which they had spied out, saying, "The land through which we have gone, in spying it out, is a land that devours its inhabitants; and all the people whom we saw in it are men of great size..."

Joshua the son of Nun and Caleb the son of Jephunneh, of those who had spied out the land, tore their clothes; and they spoke to all the congregation of the sons of Israel, saying, "The land which we passed through to spy out is an exceedingly good land. If the Lord is pleased with us, then He will bring us into this land and give it to us — a land which flows with milk and honey. Only do not rebel against the Lord; and do not fear the people of the land, for they will be our prey. Their protection has been removed from them, and the Lord is with us; do not fear them."

Numbers 13:27-33; 14:6-10

We find in this example, that operating in fear instead of faith is the second thing that will hinder a proper perspective. The ten negative spies were focusing on the giants instead of the promise. It is impossible to be in faith and in fear at the same time. You must choose, for clearly fear is the absence of faith.

We referenced faith in the last chapter, *"Faith is the substance of things hoped for..."* (Hebrews 11:1). Fear is not of God. 2 Timothy 1:7 says, *"For God hath not given us the spirit of fear; but of power, and of love, and of a sound mind"* (KJV). If we give up our hope, we will quickly start a downward spiral of fear. Joshua and Caleb chose to view the promise and did not allow the circumstances to cause fear to overtake their faith.

The third thing that can greatly affect your perspective is spiritual warfare or enemy attack. To explain this concept, I would like to share a vision the Lord gave me. The first part of the vision happened during a Sunday morning service at our church. I was on the platform singing with the praise team. The line in the song that we kept singing said, "Something's moving, something's changing..." I saw a picture of a huge grey cinderblock wall. It was a close-up view, which did not allow me to see the top, or the sides. I could see the mortar between the blocks and what I thought were small cracks forming in the mortar.

While worship continued, I began to pray about a shift I felt this represented in the Spirit. It is difficult to articulate, because it was a quick picture in my mind, but what I felt in my Spirit was huge. At this point in the service, our pastor came to the platform and began to declare to the congregation that there was a shift happening in the spirit realm. It was great confirmation for what I had just experienced. After service, I described to my pastor what I had seen. He told me that he felt there was more to come, and he would pray with me for God to reveal the rest of the vision.

That evening our congregation was invited to attend a special service at a sister church. The minister preached a message that greatly impacted me. When considering all the great examples of faith listed in Hebrews 11, I had never contemplated what is said about Joseph in verse 22.

> *By faith Joseph, when his end was near, spoke about the exodus of the Israelites from Egypt and gave instructions concerning the burial of his bones.*
> Hebrews 11:22 NIV

He provided instruction to his family that they were to take his bones with them when they went to the Promised Land. The minister said that Joseph's bones represented vision and he shared three lessons from Joseph's bones:

1. God always comes through on His Word. If He said it, it will happen!
2. A promise delayed is not a promise destroyed or denied.
3. Once you catch a glimpse of the Promised Land, you will never be content to live in Egypt!

This message was to encourage those who were ready to give up on their vision.

The journey I had been on was full of disappointments, disillusionments, and enemy attack, which had made it extremely difficult to remain focused on the vision or the destination. I was encouraged by the reminder that a delayed promise did not mean it had been destroyed or denied, but it still brought many tears. After crying the rest of that service and the hour long trip home, before going to bed, I prayed, "Lord if You really save my tears in a bottle, have You switched to a bucket yet?"

The next morning, I arose early as usual to have my personal devotion time with the Lord. I began to write in my journal about what had happened the previous day. I described the vision I had seen on the platform and the highlights of the message from the evening service. I wrote that I was aware the previous day's activities were a setup from God to help me change my perspective and focus on the destiny again. However, the reality was that my circumstances had not changed, and I could not understand how my current life was to intersect with the life I once thought I was called to live. I wrote that I felt the lines were blurred and I could not clearly see or define what God's actual promise versus my own hopes and dreams were.

I continued writing about my prayer from the previous night, "Lord if You really save my tears in a bottle, have You switched to a bucket yet?" At that moment, the vision that began the preceding day continued! Instantly I was standing in front of that cinderblock wall. This time I saw the whole wall, but it was so huge, I still could not see over it or around it. It felt like such a dry and desolate place.

Then I noticed the mortar was turning a darker grey color in between the blocks resulting from moisture. Suddenly, I was taken up high and was now looking down at the wall from an aerial view. I discovered that it was not simply a wall, but it was actually a dam! Behind the dam's wall was an enormous amount of water, which I knew was a direct result of every tear, prayer, praise, and sacrifice. It was more than a bottle or a bucket. The dam was full and pressing against the wall.

I saw myself in the water. Even though I am naturally a very strong swimmer, I was fighting with every ounce of energy to keep my head above the water. I realized that with every stroke and with every kick the water was rising higher and higher, and the force and the capacity of that river was getting greater and greater. Then I saw an empty life raft floating behind me, and I heard the Lord say to me, "This is not a passive thing! You are not to be in that raft floating aimlessly waiting for the breakthrough! This fight is purposeful!"

The view from the dam in this vision was a total perspective shift for me. I realized that where the enemy is attacking is the very place God was about to move if I would just keep fighting. Unfortunately, this is where many quit; right before the breakthrough.

We discussed in the last chapter that we have a real enemy, and his number one goal is to kill, steal, and destroy God's children. If we are in opposition to the enemy's plan, we will be in a battle as long as we are on this earth. It is very easy to allow the battle to become our focus, but God allowed me to see in this vision what was happening as a result of the battle.

My perspective changed instantly when I realized that every stroke and kick in my fight was causing the water to rise higher and higher. Additionally, the higher level was the increasing force and capacity of the river! Greater meaning came from the fact that the Lord pointed out that my battle in the water was not just a mode of survival during a storm, but a purposeful fight.

The contrast between a wall and a dam is significant. A cinderblock wall gives the idea of a dead end or an obstacle. A dam however, obstructs and controls the flow of water while creating a reservoir. A dam is a great source of power when its floodgates are opened. The greater the reservoir, the greater the power when it is released.

The enemy intends to obstruct and control the flow of God's power, but what he fails to realize is with every obstruction the reservoir is enlarging. The larger the capacity, the greater the power when released! *The greater the battle… the greater the breakthrough!*

Distraction, fear, and enemy attack are just three of the examples I gave of things that can limit our ability to perceive situations clearly. We can move to a total perspective shift when we begin to focus on the benefits of the process versus the problem. Let me provide one more analogy to drive home this point.

The contrast between a wall and a dam is similar to the one between a bridge and a tunnel. Most prefer to drive over a beautiful bridge where the scenery is visible, the sun is bright, the cell phone signal is strong, and the end is in sight. A tunnel however, can be a dark and lonely place. On my journey to transformation, there has been many times the only option for forward movement was going through a tunnel.

When you are in a tunnel, you feel isolated. I have often described these times as feeling as if I were behind glass walls. Even though I could see, I was unable to hear or feel anything. Similar to the way mobile phone signals are lost in tunnels, there was a feeling of being isolated from heaven, a feeling of not being able to hear from heaven during this season of travel. God seemed to be silent and prayers appeared to stop at the ceiling. Only the enemy's bombarding tactics echoed through this place.

Another difficulty of tunnel travel is the inability to see the end. Since tunnels are a passageway with only an entrance and an exit, they remind us of a time of waiting. Think of them like a hallway with a door at each end. Often you will find yourself in a place where the door behind you has closed but the door in front of you is still locked. You are stuck in this passageway waiting for what is next.

In between the promise and the inheritance, there is often a time of waiting. Many get off course and need a perspective shift during the times of waiting. One of the best examples found in Scripture of delayed promise is the story of Abraham.

> *The Lord said to Abram, after Lot had separated from him, "Now lift up your eyes and look from the place where you are, northward and southward and eastward and westward; for all the land which you see, I will give it to you and to your descendants forever. I will make your descendants as the dust of the earth, so that if anyone can number the dust of the earth, then your descendants can also be numbered."*
>
> Genesis 13:14-16

Abraham was promised much land for his descendants, but he was childless! The inheritance did not come quickly for Abraham. The Lord however, was faithful to remind Abraham of the promise during the waiting time (See Genesis 13:14-17; 15:1-6; 17:1-5). We learn from this story that our attitude in the tunnel or the time of waiting is critical.

> *Against all hope, Abraham in hope believed and so became the father of many nations, just as it had been said to him, "So shall your offspring be." Without weakening in his faith, he faced the fact that his body*

was as good as dead since he was about a hundred years
old and that Sarah's womb was also dead. Yet he did not
waver through unbelief regarding the promise of God,
but was strengthened in his faith and gave glory to God,
being fully persuaded that God had power to do what he
had promised.

Romans 4:18-21

The time between the promise and the inheritance was long for Abraham, but he never gave up hope. There are times that we can cause delays in the promise by our disobedience or need for course correction, but just as the minister said in his message, a promise delayed is not a promise destroyed or denied. The Bible tells us that there was a specific time for Abraham and Sarah to receive their promise. *"...At the appointed time I will return to you, at this time next year, and Sarah will have a son"* (Genesis 18:14).

One very key and often overlooked point in this story is that Abraham stepped outside the promise of God in agreement with his wife, and sought to bring God's Word to fruition by their own efforts. Abraham took Sarah's slave as his wife, and had a son called Ishmael. The Arabs are descendants of Ishmael. To this day the Arabs and the Jews have been in direct conflict with each other, and it is predicted that they both will come face to face in a final battle in the last days. Imagine that. Abraham failed to wait for the fulfillment of God's promise and initiated a 4,000 year war between two half-brothers that will culminate in the end times.

There is an appointed time for your promise to be fulfilled. Do not become oppressed by the enemy and become victim to his lies, causing God's plans to be put on hold. We can be blinded or have our vision and perspective altered by victim mentality. When this occurs, we become more confident in

Satan's strategies on the earth being successful than in God's plan coming to fruition.

How were the individuals we used as examples different? What made Mary, Joshua, Caleb, and Abraham different? They placed priority on their relationship with God. Our relationship with God will determine our perspective. Our perspective will control our decisions. Our decisions will define our destiny.

Chapter 7

ARE WE THERE YET?

Last year I was traveling to our lake home with my two grandsons. We had not driven very far when I heard the four-year-old, the one who had given me my special grandma name, say, "Namry, how many more miles until we get there?" I did not think much about my response and just answered that is was about 90 miles. After about five minutes of travel, I heard from the backseat, "Namry, how many miles now?" Since my car has a screen in the dash with a visible GPS map, I quickly set it to our destination address, and the voice said we had 90 miles to travel. My smart grandson quickly reminded me that I had told him that amount five minutes ago! For the next two hours, there were frequent questions from the backseat about how many more miles were left on the screen. Soon the two-year old grandson had learned how to ask this question too. I decided that the best solution was a distraction. I taught them the game called "I Spy," and we took turns describing the things that we could see on the journey.

This is what I have endeavored to do throughout the previous chapters. I have described things that have been revealed to me along the journey. First, we learned that storms are inevitable, but our response to the storm is critical. There was a huge storm raging when Peter stepped out of that boat onto the water. As long as he kept his focus on Jesus, the storm was uneventful. He sank when he became distracted by the storm. There is a place in the "eye" of the storm where there is perfect peace and calm. Jesus is the "I AM" of the storm. If you will keep your focus on Him and allow your perspective to be guided by His promises, you will not sink.

We also talked much about obstacles, roadblocks, and detours. If you truly love, you open yourself up to be hurt deeply. Likewise, if you live a life full of hope and expectation, there is an opportunity to feel disappointed and disillusioned. It is worth the risk! Love empowers us to live life outside of our human propensities (see 1 Corinthians 13). David said in Psalm 39:7(AMP), *"And now, Lord, what do I wait for and expect? My hope and expectation are in You."* I am convinced the Father responds when we live in anticipation full of love and hope! Let me share one last Word from the Lord our church received that describes this idea well:

> *"The Lord knows the path that you are on. He knows the road that you have taken. He knows the feeling of your infirmities and the afflictions, because the Lord has walked that road and has been on that path. But the Lord has gone before you, and He will lead you and He will direct you and He will never separate Himself from you. It is by faith that you walk in this journey. It is not by sight. You do not look at the things that are before you as those things that will overcome you, but rather you look at those things that are before you as the challenge that the Holy Spirit has equipped you for. And He has anointed you and enabled you to be strong. He has enabled you and anointed you to His purposes. So be not*

weary in doing well and be not weary in walking the journey, and do not give into the devices of the flesh, and to the desires of the flesh. But if you will remain faithful, He will do as He has promised. He will bring to pass those things that He has spoken to you through His Word, and in your spirit those things that He has given to you, He will bring to pass those things. His Word to you will not return void. It will accomplish the purpose for which it was sent.

Trust in the Lord and do good and wait patiently upon Him, and do not fret because of the circumstances that you find yourself in. For the Lord is leading you from victory to victory. It has been written 'The just shall live by faith.' The words are unalterable, they are unchanging. 'The just shall live by faith,' and you will be justified by your work and by your walk. As you walk in the spirit, you will look back and see that the Lord has been good and the Lord has been faithful. And you will join that cloud of witnesses for those that witness of the Lord are those who have walked through the valley of difficulties and have seen the hand of the Lord miraculously provide, and have seen the faithfulness of the Lord. And it is He who has given you life, it is He who has given you strength, it is He who gives you hope for now and for eternity. So trust in the Lord and wait patiently upon Him and follow after Him and He will lead you into greener pastures, and to a time of restoration and in times of refreshing, and you will know that the Lord, He is your God!"

It is important to be able to recognize the hazards that can get us off the desired course, because it allows us to guard against their hindering of our forward momentum. As we have discovered, there are opportunities on the road for some pace changes and delays, but there are also openings to jump into the fast lane and drive forward until our reality and our destiny collide!

How do we get into the fast lane? I believe it starts with relationship. Being loved and having a sense of belonging is essential to our basic human needs. The best way to meet this need is through intimate relationships. The most powerful relationship in your life should be with your Lord and Savior! Loving Him and loving people is the ultimate level of true righteousness.

A healthy relationship requires some key elements. Some of these are love, communication, transparency, and accountability. When we open ourselves up through these attributes, we develop an intimate relationship that becomes the basis for our confidence, faith, and trust in the other party.

Individuals have an opportunity to share their relationship status on social media. I wonder what people would think if they saw a post that stated, "Rhonda is in a relationship with Jesus!" Most are comfortable sharing other associations publicly, but I dare say this post would be unusual. However, this relationship should be our highest priority. It should be based on the key elements of all healthy relationships and should grow as we spend more time in His presence.

> *...For whoever would come near to God must [necessarily] believe that God exists and that He is the rewarder of those who earnestly and diligently seek Him [out].*
> Hebrews 11:6 AMP

There is a void inside of you which can only be satisfied with a personal relationship with your Savior. I believe if we diligently seek Him by making room for Him in our lives, and by developing a place to host His presence, we will find the most fulfilling relationship available. We will literally experience heaven on earth.

Consider Moses as an example. We learned in a previous chapter that he was transformed during an encounter with the presence of God, and then he developed an intimate relationship with God. God communed with Moses as a friend would commune with us. Ultimately, out of that relationship came very specific instructions for how to make a place for worship to God (See Exodus 25-27). The tabernacle or "Tent of Meeting" was the first place that was built to host the presence of God. It was a sanctuary or a place set apart for the Lord to dwell and meet with His people.

> "This shall be a continual burnt offering throughout your generations at the door of the Tent of Meeting before the Lord, where I will meet with you to speak there to you. There I will meet with the Israelites, and the Tent of Meeting shall be sanctified by My glory [the Shekinah, God's visible presence]. And I will sanctify the Tent of Meeting and the altar; I will sanctify also both Aaron and his sons to minister to Me in the priest's office. And I will dwell among the Israelites and be their God. And they shall know [from personal experience] that I am the Lord their God, Who brought them forth out of the land of Egypt that I might dwell among them; I am the Lord their God."
>
> Exodus 29:42-46 AMP

First, Moses did his part by following the instructions that were provided. As a result, God did His part!

...So Moses finished the work. Then the cloud [the Shekinah, God's visible presence] covered the Tent of Meeting, and the glory of the Lord filled the tabernacle! And Moses was not able to enter the Tent of Meeting because the cloud remained upon it, and the glory of the Lord filled the tabernacle.

Exodus 40:33b-35 AMP

David was the second example we previously considered. He also understood the importance of making a place for the Lord to dwell. David was responsible for getting the Ark of the Covenant back to the tabernacle after it had been stolen. He then received instructions about building a temple to replace the Tent of Meeting (See 2 Samuel 6-7). Although David had in his heart to build the temple, God instructed him that it was his seed that would carry out the mandate. So David paved the way for his son Solomon, who was ultimately responsible for completing the instructions. Once again, when they were faithful to do their part, God did His.

...in unison when the trumpeters and the singers were to make themselves heard with one voice to praise and to glorify the Lord, and when they lifted up their voice accompanied by trumpets and cymbals and instruments of music, and when they praised the Lord saying, "He indeed is good for His lovingkindness is everlasting," then the house, the house of the Lord, was filled with a cloud, so that the priests could not stand to minister because of the cloud, for the glory of the Lord filled the house of God. Then Solomon said, "The Lord has said that He would dwell in the thick cloud. I have built You a lofty house, and a place for Your dwelling forever."'

2 Chronicles 5:13-6:2

R h o n d a   B a r n e s

The same concept was true for the New Testament believers and is still true for us today, but in even greater measure. When Jesus died on the cross, the Bible says the veil in the temple was torn in two from top to bottom (Matthew 27:51). Jesus provided the means for us to become the temple! God no longer dwelt in houses made by human hands.

> "Or do you not know that your body is a temple of the Holy Spirit who is in you, whom you have from God, and that you are not your own? For you have been bought with a price: therefore glorify God in your body."
>
> 1 Corinthians 6:19-20

There were divisions in the original tabernacle. The priests performed their ritual acts of worship in one part. However, only once a year was the high priest allowed to go beyond the veil into the Holy of Holies (See Hebrews 9). Jesus made a better way for us. Now this is available to all, not just a high priest!

> But when Christ appeared as a high priest of the good things to come, He entered through the greater and more perfect tabernacle, not made with hands, that is to say, not of this creation; and not through the blood of goats and calves, but through His own blood, He entered the holy place once for all, having obtained eternal redemption...
>
> For Christ did not enter a holy place made with hands, a mere copy of the true one, but into heaven itself, now to appear in the presence of God for us...
>
> Therefore, brethren, since we have confidence to enter the holy place by the blood of Jesus, by a new and living way which He inaugurated for us through the veil, that is, His flesh, and since we have a great priest over the

house of God, let us draw near with a sincere heart in
full assurance of faith, having our hearts sprinkled clean
from an evil conscience and our bodies washed with pure
water. Let us hold fast the confession of our hope without
wavering, for He who promised is faithful; and let us
consider how to stimulate one another to love and good
deeds, not forsaking our own assembling together, as is
the habit of some, but encouraging one another; and all
the more as you see the day drawing near.

Hebrews 9:11-13; 24; 10: 19-25

Under the old covenant, the people responded to the presence of God with fear and trembling. Only Moses approached God on Mount Sinai (See Exodus 19-20). Now, because of the price Jesus paid, we can come boldly and enter the holy place. If we do our part, He will do His!

But you are a chosen people, a royal priesthood, a holy
nation, God's special possession, that you may declare
the praises of him who called you out of darkness into his
wonderful light.

1 Peter 2:9 NIV

We can make a place for Him to inhabit. I call this my secret place. I strongly believe we need both an individual secret place, and a corporate one. There are times that our relationship with God requires dedicated individual one-on-one time together. There are also realms in God which are more easily accessed through a joined faith with other believers.

"Again I say to you, that if two of you agree on earth
about anything that they may ask, it shall be done for

them by My Father who is in heaven. For where two or
three have gathered together in My name, I am there in
their midst."

Matthew 18:19-20

In order for our relationship with our Lord and Savior to grow, there are two things we should do in both a personal and corporate setting. We should learn to host His presence and usher in His glory.

When I think about being a host, it means I am either entertaining guests or providing a space for an event. If I am preparing to host guests at my home for dinner, I prepare a place and a meal for them. It is a very deliberate plan. Depending on the circumstances, I may make extra room at the table. I prepare dishes that I seldom use for routine meals. After the meal, we often find pleasure in just sitting around the table to fellowship.

If we would approach our time with the Lord with this same mentality, we would reap substantially. While I do not believe in legalistic spiritual habits, I do feel a deliberate plan is crucial. Most can easily say that they are too busy, but we find time for the things that are important to us. If you will set aside a specific time each day to spend in "Spirit-led" prayer, Bible study, and worship, you will find He will meet you there. In this place, you begin to host His presence and these disciplines no longer are a duty, they become a delight! Some days the Holy Spirit might direct you to spend more time studying, other days there may be a specific unction for more prayer. At times, you may worship and there may need to be moments of complete silence. Make room, designate time, and be patient in His presence and allow Him to direct the activity.

I believe that this advice applies to our corporate gatherings as well. We often refer to these times as worship services, and sadly, we often have an agenda that does not allow time for true worship, which invites His presence. We also see group prayer services where there is actually very little prayer. Imagine what could happen if we could move past man's plans and make our gatherings all about Him! Every service should flow out of a priority of hosting His presence. From this place, our worship, prayer, and preaching would have greater power and we would see the world change!

The second thing we must do to cultivate our relationship with God is to usher in His glory. When I studied the word "usher," I learned that it comes from a word that means doorkeeper. It is closely related to the word forerunner or harbinger, which is a term for a pioneer or someone who initiates major change (*Merriam-Webster's Collegiate Dictionary*, 2005).

Jesus was our ultimate forerunner. He came to this earth in human form and overcame every temptation known to man. He was a pioneer. During His short time of ministry on the earth, He performed many miracles, signs, and wonders for the glory of God. However, He said we are to do even greater things!

> *"Truly, truly, I say to you, he who believes in Me, the works that I do, he will do also; and greater works than these he will do; because I go to the Father. Whatever you ask in My name, that will I do, so that the Father may be glorified in the Son. If you ask Me anything in My name, I will do it."*
>
> John 14:12-14

Rhonda Barnes

If Jesus said this, why then should we be content with doing far less? I want to be part of the "Greater Things Club!" When we usher in God's glory all things become possible. We begin to function from the place of authority He provided for us that we previously reviewed in the first chapter of Ephesians. This scripture reminds us that the same power that was exerted to raise Christ from the dead is available to Christians today. It also describes the authority He provided for His church. From this realm, we are stretched to embrace the words of the Lord's Prayer, *"Your kingdom come. Your will be done, on earth as it is in heaven"* (Matthew 6:10). There is no sickness, inadequacies, or lack in heaven. I believe it is possible that when we usher in God's glory, these things cannot exist in the earth for those who will believe! One thing to note here as well, is that the absence of miracles or the Glory of God may not be directly related to a lack of faith, but the presence of unbelief. Faith and unbelief can co-exist but it renders us powerless. We must seek God to eradicate unbelief from our lives.

In closing, I would like to share a dream that also summarizes these concepts. In my dream, I was moving from a small house to a larger one a short distance away. My husband had solicited help from others to pack things in preparation for moving. When I arrived, they were not working but were all seated in the room and visiting, but said that things were ready to move. However, when I walked through the house, there were many things not packed, and junk that needed to be thrown away. The more I moved, the more I found! I was trying to organize and was expecting my friend to come to assist, but when she arrived, she told me that she needed to go somewhere else. I was frustrated at this last-minute change, but I kept working. Then my husband came into the room and said, "We cannot move forward because we do not have the keys to the new place we are moving to!" I awoke at this point.

Later, after I was asleep again, I had a second dream. In this dream, I was interpreting the first dream. I knew that moving from the smaller house to the larger one was symbolic to moving forward to the next level, or the next thing God had for us. The fact that my husband and his friends had sat down, instead of preparing to move, represented a spirit of complacency, lethargy, and mediocrity that is present in many Christian's lives and in the church. Organizing things and getting rid of junk was figurative of what we must lose to move forward. All the bondages and limitations that hold us captive must go! I also knew that my friend telling me she had to do something else at the last minute represented the spirit of distraction that is trying to prevent forward movement. Lastly, no keys symbolized our inability to receive the keys God has made available to us to allow forward momentum.

The new place was there, in view, but there were things that had to be done in order to be able to occupy it! Jesus has provided all the keys for us to inhabit our place of destiny. We must contend for it!

> And Jacob was left alone, and a Man wrestled with him until daybreak. And when [the Man] saw that He did not prevail against [Jacob], He touched the hollow of his thigh; and Jacob's thigh was put out of joint as he wrestled with Him. Then He said, "Let Me go, for day is breaking." But [Jacob] said, "I will not let You go unless You declare a blessing upon me." [The Man] asked him, "What is your name?" And [in shock of realization, whispering] he said, "Jacob" [supplanter, schemer, trickster, swindler]! And He said, "Your name shall be called no more Jacob [supplanter], but Israel [contender

with God]; for you have contended and have power with God and with men and have prevailed." Then Jacob asked Him, "Tell me, I pray You, what [in contrast] is Your name?" But He said, "Why is it that you ask My name?" And [the Angel of God declared] a blessing on [Jacob] there. And Jacob called the name of the place Peniel [the face of God], saying, For I have seen God face to face, and my life is spared and not snatched away. And as he passed Peniel, the sun rose upon him, and he was limping because of his thigh.

Genesis 32:24-31 AMP

Jacob contended for God's glory! Jacob walked down a road of transformation, and became a new man. His very name was changed. During his time of wrestling, he had to respond to the question, "What is your name?" I believe this question is very similar to the question Elijah was asked in the cave, "Why are you here?" It was an opportunity for some soul searching. Jacob had to determine if he was going to continue living the life his name defined. He had to decide if he would continue to deceive himself and others; or if he was finally ready to allow God to transform him. After the severe struggle, his heart and his character were both transformed. The changing of his name sealed the process! In the beginning, Jacob was a deceiver but after the struggle, his name was changed because he was a contender with God! Hosea 12:3 says about Jacob, *"In the womb...took his brother by the heel, and in his maturity he contended with God."* That name change signified a new beginning, but the experience left him with a limp.

Your journey may have caused scars as well. The storms that you have driven through may have caused a limp, which is a constant reminder of the reality of loss and the frailty of life. I want to share something I wrote in my journal during my personal journey:

> "Many days I feel less than adequate and a disappointment to God. I have concern that my wrong decisions have reset my destiny and now I am stuck traveling a road which is going the wrong direction. Other days I feel like it is all just a dream – the destiny I thought I was to walk in is just a storybook life I created in my own mind. On a few days, I see what I think God sees, and I am who He says I am.
>
> I need to turn those few days into all my days and live life 'unlocked' and never allow my identity to be stolen again!"

This entry in my journal shows how in our human emotions, we are subject to feelings that do not line up with God's truth. Guard your heart and always let the promises of God's Word take priority over your feelings and emotions. Do not allow yourself to be stuck, and do not pull off the road! Move forward past all the obstacles, past transition and into transformation! It is not about the road, it is about the journey. When I am driving into the small town where I reside, my GPS will say, "Your destination is straight ahead." As long as you continue on the road, you will be transformed from glory to glory until you pass from this life to the next one in eternity.

While you are here, contend for a piece of heaven on earth, but more importantly, live your life in a way that assures you spend eternity with Christ. Heaven is an amazing place and I want to meet all of you there someday!

REFERENCES

Faith. (1995). In *Strong's exhaustive concordance: New American standard Bible*. (Updated ed.). Retrieved from http://www.biblestudytools.com/concordances/strongs-exhaustive-concordance/

Jesus Culture. (2010). My soul longs for you [Recorded by Jesus Culture]. On *Come away [CD]*. Sacramento, CA: Jesus Culture Music (2010)

McAlmon, T. (2005). How we need the river [Recorded by T. McAlmon]. On *The glory of his presence* [CD]. Colorado Springs, CO: McAlmon Music, LLC (2005)

Merriam-Webster's collegiate dictionary (11th ed.). (2005). Springfield, MA: Merriam-Webster.

Morgan, R. & Zschech, D. (2011). *Believe* [Recorded by Hillsong]. On *A Beautiful Exchange [CD]. Sydney, AU: EMI (2010)*

Revival. (2009). In *Microsoft Encarta Dictionary*. Retrieved from http://encarta.msn.com/encnet/features/dictionary/dictionaryhome.aspx

Transfigured. 2014. In *Merriam-Webster.com*. Retrieved November 3, 2014, from http://www.merriam-webster.com/dictionary/transfigured

For speaking opportunities about the book,
please contact:

rhondabarnes@embarqmail.com
573-729-8171

Made in the USA
San Bernardino, CA
16 November 2014